USHERING

in

HIS PRESENCE

USHERING *in* HIS PRESENCE

A MANUAL FOR CHRISTIAN USHERS

Celestine S. Ikwuamaesi

SAVINGWORD PUBLISHERS

© 2004 by Celestine S. Ikwuamaesi

All rights reserved. No part of this publication may be reproduced in any form without written permission from SavingWord Publishers, P. O. Box 54781, Ikoyi Lagos Nigeria.
email <*celestineikwuamaesi@yahoo.com*>

ISBN   1-59457-873-7

Unless otherwise identified, all Scripture quotations in this publication are taken from the King James Version (KJ).
Other Scripture quotations are identified as follows:
The New King James Version (NKJV).
The New International Version (NIV).
The Living Bible (TLB).
New Living Translation (NLT).
Letters to the Young Churches (J B Phillips).

Published in USA by BookSurge, LLC for SavingWord Publishers.
To order additional copies, please contact
BookSurge, LLC
www.booksurge.com
1-866-308-6235
orders@booksurge.com

To Glad, who "prophesied" me into ushering;
To late Pastor Adetola, who "conscripted" me into ushering;
To the Full Gospel Business Men's Fellowship International, Lagos Area Chapters, that gave me the chance to minister at large audience meetings;
To my daughter, Onyeka, who took up the baton.

Other publication by Celestine S. Ikwuamaesi

Time for Relevance
(BookSurge, LLC, 2004)

CONTENTS

Acknowledgments		9
Introduction		11

PART 1: THE MEANING OF USHERING

Chapter One	Biblical Basis of Ushering	17
Chapter Two	Perception of Ushering	25
Chapter Three	Psychology of Ushering	33
Chapter Four	Preparation for Ushering	39

PART 2: BUILDING THE TEAM

Chapter Five	Every Church Needs a Team	49
Chapter Six	The Head Usher	53
Chapter Seven	The Training Process	63

PART 3: USHERING IN ACTION

Chapter Eight	General Principles	71

Chapter Nine	The Local Church	75
Chapter Ten	Large - Scale Ushering	85
Chapter Eleven	Ushering At The Car Park	105

Part 4: WRAPPING UP

Chapter Twelve	Spiritual Warfare for Ushers	113
Chapter Thirteen	Benefits of Ushering	127
Chapter Fourteen	Problems Of Ushering	133
Chapter Fifteen	Usher's Quick Reference	137
Notes		149

ACKNOWLEDGEMENTS

A finished book is the work of more than one person, a combined effort of many contributors. *Ushering In His Presence* is no exception. One person planted the idea in my mind; another person "set me up" for the idea to become real; another exploded the idea into reality; another tracked the evolution of the writing process with proofing and suggestions; yet others gave moral backing and encouragement.

I appreciate all these efforts. They arose from an inspired desire to see decency and order in the Lord's work. I should, therefore, thank all the wonderful people who labored with me in the ushering ministry both in the Redeemed Christian Church of God (Victoria Island/Ikoyi) and the Full Gospel Business Men's Fellowship International (Lagos Area Chapters). Appreciation also goes to Mr. Emma Okoronkwo for his encouragement and to Mr. Imohimi

Ozoya for his wonderful editorial input. My wife, Glad, not only "prophesied me into the ministry" but also deployed her ushering experience to help shape the form of this book.

Finally, I thank my publishers, BookSurge, LLC who, through their professional strictness with my earlier work, gave me a peep into the technical intricacies of book writing and publishing in an electronic age.

INTRODUCTION

I laughed hilariously as we settled down at the lunch table one Sunday afternoon. "Be an usher? You must be kidding!" I managed to say.

"Just give it a thought. But on your knees, of course. Though I think it's a good idea as I leave for the praise group."

"Look, Glad, you know I don't have the knack for ushering; what with the stress, the walking about, and the spotlighting and glamor."

Shortly after, in September 1993, my wife's suggestion turned out indeed a prophecy when my pastor 'conscripted' me to head the ushering department. The church had just ordained the former head usher and posted him out to pastor a new parish. With no prior ushering experience behind me and no literature materials to have recourse to, I saw the assignment as a huge task.

The first two Sunday worship services were a harrowing experience as my legs wobbled with long standing and walking about. I almost gave up, not knowing that I was going through an 'initiation'. However, my attitude changed before long. I discovered that I had joined a ministry that is dear to God's heart and fundamental to sound Christian life. It offered me an opportunity to serve others and, consequently, my experience later turned out to confirm Charles Sibthorpe's statement,

> One of the key principles of leadership is the willingness to be a servant. The quality of every potential leader will be tested and trained through the simple, even menial, tasks which he is asked to do.[1]

Early in 1996, the Full Gospel Business Men's Fellowship International (FGBMFI), Lagos Area Chapters, appointed me to head the Ushering Sub-Committee for her September Lagos Regional Convention. I was to mobilize ushers from different Chapters of the Fellowship and build up a team to minister at the Convention.

I went on my knees in prayer and the Lord gave me a training guideline that I developed, taught, and demonstrated during series of meetings. The result was a successful ushering at the Convention. On reviewing the performance of the ushers, I felt the need to develop the guideline into a manual for the ushering ministry to the benefit of the church. There was an initial delay in publishing the manual, but this paid off when, once again, the Fellowship called me to handle her 1999 West Africa Regional Convention. This offered me an opportunity to organize the ushers for a convention of wider scale and size, and to field-test the principles in this book.

Ushering In His Presence, therefore, derives from practical experience both at the local church level and at nondenominational largescale meetings. It should serve as a manual for ushers and as a resource material for the church. The book focuses on developing ushering principles that should apply to any situation. It brings out the importance and spirituality of the ministry and how it could tune up the spiritual level of Christian meetings. Consequently, the book has a universal appeal because it addresses a common enemy, the spirit that causes disorder and confusion at Christian meetings.

Ushering In His Presence contains fifteen chapters, which are in four parts. Part one defines the meaning and content of ushering and explains the biblical bases for the ministry. It further shows the necessary preparations that should help an usher make a success of the ministry.

Part two focuses on the development of a strong ushering team, suggests a typical structure for a team, and explains the role of the head usher. It further explains how to recruit, train, and harmonize a group of people into a functional spirit-filled team. Part three discusses the functioning of the ministry, explaining the necessary preparations for an outing and the actual ministering during meetings. It concludes with a chapter on ushering at the car park, a recognition of the place the motor car in modern culture.

Finally, part four deals with issues of general interest, with emphasis on spiritual warfare and benefits of ushering. It concludes with a quick reference guide, an on-thefly review of the entire book.

As the name implies, the main focus of this book is on ushering at Christian meetings, whether church services, evangelistic crusades, or conventions. A good material for Christian workers in the ministry of ushering, it is written in simple flowing language. Therefore, it should appeal to ushers with different cultural and educational backgrounds.

I pray that the great teacher, the Holy Spirit, would enable such workers to benefit from the eternal purpose of this book.

Celestine S. Ikwuamaesi
Lagos, Nigeria
August 2004

PART 1
THE MEANING OF USHERING

The world *'USHER'* refers to a person who shows people to their seats in a cinema, church, and public hall. It also means a 'Doorkeeper', a person that stands at the door to let people in and out. In this sense, ushering is the process of directing people at large gathering, starting from keeping the door to leading them to their seats. However, it goes beyond the narrow dictionary meaning. It involves all it takes to make a gathering a success, ensuring order by taking control of events before and during the program. Since the focus of this book is on ushering at Christian functions, it is good to refer to the Bible, which has a lot to say about ushering.

1
BIBLICAL BASIS OF USHERING

The Bible reveals that there was confusion and disorder on earth before God created the physical things we see. But when He spoke light into the world, order set in and life started to develop.

And the earth was without form, and void; and darkness was upon the face of the deep. And the Spirit of God moved upon the face of the waters. And God said, Let there be light: and there was light. (Genesis 1:2-3)

Order is vital to life, growth, and development. For example, the existence of order led to man's coming together in an organized fashion to build a tower that would reach the heavens. The people were mobilized, organized, and motivated to embark on a communal project.

> *And they said, Go to, let us build us a city and a tower, whose top may reach unto heaven; and let us make us a name, lest we be scattered abroad upon the face of the whole earth. (Genesis 11:4)*

Ushering is not a product of modern society. It has been in existence ever since man learned to get together for common social functions. Therefore, as an integral part of man's social evolution, ushering turned more sophisticated as society grew more complex. Evidence of this assertion is everywhere in the Bible where there are lots of references to events that attracted crowds. Both in the wilderness and when the people settled as a nation, there were instances of large gatherings to deliberate on issues affecting their common interest. The orderly conduct of such meetings [there is no biblical account of any serious disorder] indicate the practice of ushering. In reference to such gatherings the Psalmist says that he would rather be a doorkeeper in the court of the Lord than to dwell in the tents of wickedness.

> *For a day in thy courts is better than a thousand. I had rather be a doorkeeper in the house of my God, than to dwell in the tents of wickedness. (Psalm 84:10)*

A court is a place where large crowds of people gather. There has to be persons whose role is to maintain order at such gatherings. These are the ushers.

USHERING IN THE MINISTRY OF CHRIST

Our Lord organized series of public meetings during His earthly ministry. Though there is no biblical record that He had an ushering team that worked with Him, there was order in each of the public meetings. This means that the disciples might have served as ushers and rendered all the needed help. The same assertion holds for the ministry of the first century church. In effect, what happened during the Lord's ministry and at the Pentecost should help us appreciate the place of ushering in church life. Ushering, irrespective of its scale, is an essential part of Christian teamwork.

Healing Sessions

The Lord conducted several healing sessions, which evidently attracted large crowds of people. There is no record of disorder at any of such meetings except the case of the healing of the paralytic (Mark 2:15).

In this case, poor ushering made it possible for the friends of the paralytic to gain access to the Lord's presence in a very unusual way. Though the whole incident speaks of faith on the part of the paralytic and his friends, it equally reflects the quality of ushering. One can imagine the level of distraction this strange approach might have caused at the meeting. One equally wonders what the ushers were doing when the people started climbing the roof top. A lot can happen at a meeting whenever the ushers lose concentration on the goings-on.

Feeding of 5000 People

Our Lord fed about 5000 people with five loaves of bread and two fishes. He asked the disciples to make the people sit down in manageable groups of 50s and 100s. They distributed the food, gathered the leftover, and took record of the number of people that fed from the provision. The disciples served as ushers.

> *Breaking the loaves into pieces, he kept giving the bread and fish to the disciples to give to the people ... and they picked up twelve baskets of leftover bread and fish. (Mark 6:41-43 NLT)*

Visit By Members of His Family

Christ was teaching a large group when His mother and His brothers visited. One of the disciples [playing the role of ushers] informed Him of the visit without disrupting His teaching.

> *While he yet talked to the people, behold, his mother and his brethren stood without, desiring to speak with him. Then one said unto him, Behold, thy mother and thy brethren stand without, desiring to speak with thee. (Matthew 12:46-50)*

Damsel At The Door

The Bible records that when the Jewish officials took the Lord to the High Priest, one of His disciples spoke to a young lady that kept the door [an usher] before she allowed Peter into the palace.

But Peter stood at the door without. Then went out that other disciple, which was known unto the high priest, and spake unto her that kept the door, and brought in Peter. (John 18:16)

The Seven Deacons

The influence of the Holy Spirit brought about massive growth of the early church. The apostles contained the problem of the sudden growth by appointing seven deacons. These took charge of daily serving of tables while they [disciples] focused on teaching the Christian doctrines. Primarily, the seven served as ushers. Their being appointed through prayer underscores the spiritual significance of ushering in the church.

Wherefore, brethren, look ye out among you seven men of honest report, full of the Holy Ghost and wisdom, whom we may appoint over this business. (Acts 6:3)

When God appoints a leader for kingdom service, He raises men and women to support the person. Therefore, ushering is a helps ministry God set up to enhance the operations of the church.

> *And God hath set some in the church, first apostles, secondarily prophets, thirdly teachers, after that miracles, then gifts of healings, helps, governments, diversities of tongues. (1 Corinthians 12:28)*

Helps ministry existed right from the biblical times, in the church in the wilderness. For example, when Moses protested against the calling to deliver the people of God on the basis of his perceived natural limitations, God appointed Aaron to assist him. Again, when the responsibility of administering a nation in transit weighed heavily on Moses, God appointed men to help him. These may not necessarily be ushers but they provided the needed help to the man of God, Moses.

> *And I will come down and talk with thee there: and I will take of the spirit which is upon thee, and will put it upon them; and they shall bear the burden of the people with thee, that thou bear it not thyself alone. (Numbers 11:17)*

We should, however, note that the name, 'helps' does not imply a subordinate ministry. In kingdom work, every role counts and contributes to the overall success of the divine purpose. No segment of ministry work will succeed without order and harmony in its operations. Since order and harmony are dear to God, He has raised the ushering ministry to help the church carry out its work. Ushering is God's heartbeat, and an intending ushers should bear this spiritual fact in mind and see his or her role as a vital aspect of church ministry.

WHY DO WE USHER?

We mentioned at the beginning that order is an attribute of God. He infused it in all works of creation, and therefore, disorder cannot come from God. The Bible says:

"… for God is not a God of disorder but of harmony, as is plain in all the Churches." (I Corinthians 14:33 [J.B.Phillips])

This Scripture implies that since God does not like disorder or confusion, then the devil does. So, whenever Christians gather in the name of Jesus Christ, the devil would endeavor to introduce disorder. Thus, a Christian gathering should need spiritually sound ushering for a smooth operation. This holds true for every meeting, irrespective of its size and the level of spirituality, and the social and intellectual maturity of the people at the meeting. In effect, sound ushering is mandatory, or else, the purpose of the meeting would be lost. Therefore, we usher for various reasons.

Orderly Conduct

The Lord promises to be in the midst of a group that gathers in His name. This promise is conditional; the purpose of the gathering must glorify Jesus. However, it is not possible to know every person's motive for coming to a function. So, the organizers of the meeting set the rules for the function; ushering ensures that people conform to the set rules.

Success of A Program

There is a purpose for every meeting and it shows when the program ends successfully within the planned time frame. Ushering ensures that the roles of those involved blend smoothly to achieve the desired goal.

Effective Participation

A Christian meeting is all-involving. A meeting is spiritually successful if it runs smoothly with good timing and orderliness; if it enables the people to participate as they should. Good ushering enhances effective participation of both the organizers and the attendee.

Safety of Life And Property

People who come to Christian meetings do not expect to get hurt, or lose their personal effects. Ushers help them realize this desire by keeping watch over personal effects and managing the crowd in time of emergencies. They provide a safe atmosphere for everyone to play their roles.

2
PERCEPTION OF USHERING

The strain of standing all through functions scared me and, as a result, I never took interest in ushering. Besides, I thought it was all about walking around, directing people to their seats, and basking in the glamor of the spotlight. This perception, coupled with my natural dislike for high visibility in the church, made me feel quite unfit for the ministry.

However, these views changed immensely a couple of months after I started ushering. First, I discovered that ushers are not born but made by training and experience. Some innate qualities—those natural qualities which one exhibits effortlessly—could stand one out as a good candidate for the ministry. But they complement the training and experience to produce a well-rounded usher. Second, I discovered that it takes more than physical appearance and fitness to be an usher. The ministry has three key dimensions to it: the spiritual, the psychological, and the physical. An usher should prepare in these areas.

Some people may have the potential but are put off by the physical and psychological demands of ushering. It is advisable that an intending usher should first, confirm the divine call into the ministry, identify his or her potential, and then move on by faith.

Let's identify these potentials by running through the following self-assessment questions:

1. Do you love helping others?
2. Do you like order in your personal life?
3. Do you bother about your personal appearance at public meetings?
4. Are you an extrovert—you easily mix with new persons?
5. How do you react when a meeting does not run smoothly?
6. Do you like taking initiative to ensure that things function well in the church?
7. Is there a subtle urge in you toward ushering?

The feeling of God's call is the most important thing to watch out for. All other attributes come with time, training, and practice. When He calls one into a specific ministry, He makes the one willing and able to function in it. But a problem arises when the individual disregards the Holy Spirit and does the work through his personal efforts and experience. The Bible says,

For it is God which worketh in you both to will and to do of his good pleasure. (Philippians 2:13)

QUALITIES OF AN USHER

We know that the holy Spirit plays a significant role in every aspect of God's work yet everyone does not fit into every ministry. Some are naturally prepared by God to operate in His determined areas of church work. There are, therefore, certain qualities that distinguish God's workers and this enables them to fit easily into their slot. What then are these qualities?

Self-image

The usher is a doorkeeper in the court of the King of kings, Jesus Christ. So, his self-image should show in his poise, carriage, confidence, and the relaxed but firm approach to handling issues. Self-image shapes and projects the usher's personality and makes him radiate love and sharpness of mind. These reflect in the character and quality of his ushering and endears him to the congregation. The air of confidence does not come from a worldly pride or from a feeling of self-accomplishment. It rather comes from an inward peace of a worker that is conscious of his or her relationship with the Holy Spirit. It is a humbling type of peace.

Humor

An usher should have a good sense of humor. This

enables him get around some difficult situations when dealing with people. But display of humor should flow naturally, timely, and relevantly to specific situations. Consequently, it relaxes stressed up people who, ordinarily, should be sulky and low beat because of some personal problems. Apart from working on others, humor relaxes the usher and allows him the room to creatively find solutions to problems.

I came across a woman at one of the international conventions in Lagos. Apparently stressed from a long drive from the countryside, she resisted the ushers' attempt to move her from the reserved seating area. By the time I got to her, others were watching to see the outcome of the face off. After smiling at her, I announced to the hearing of all that I was co-opting her into the ushering team; her duty was to ensure that nobody occupied the reserved seats until I could find her an alternative seat. There was laughter everywhere. She had expected a bossy bellow but got a relaxing surprise. Within five minutes, she vacated the seat for the place the ushers had earlier intended.

Appearance

There is a popular saying that a man is his own best advertisement. The usher is both a 'sales representative' and a 'public relations officer' of his church or Christian organization. His appearance tells a lot of story about his person, the organization, and the quality of the meeting. Good appearance here covers dressing, carriage, and comportment. It does not depend on how costly one's dressing is, but on the general neatness that reflects a wholesome personality and Christian decency.

Dressing should reflect the general dress culture of the society. For example, the type of tight fitting dresses some female ushers wear in Europe could cause uproar in an African Christian gathering. In such a case, the usher's mode of dressing could distract others and negatively affect their participation at a meeting. It could even hurt the conscience of some spiritually weak ones by leading them to unwholesome thoughts, and thus affect the general spiritual atmosphere of a meeting. Some years back, the visit of an American female minister coincided with our pastor's series of teachings on the covering of the hair. The series was concluded at the Sunday morning service and the visiting minister came to officiate in the evening without covering her hair. She had one hour preaching time but left after struggling for about 20 minutes because she could not communicate. It follows that an usher's appearance could have positive or negative impact on the congregation.

The head usher can prescribe a dress code if it will help him maintain a good level of discipline within the team. Having a common dress code is good because it serves as a 'leveller' for both the glamorous and the shy, and the rich and the poor. Whichever dress pattern, ushers should not be unduly conscious of their dressing; but should be decently noticeable in the congregation.

Personal Hygiene

The usher's personal hygiene matters a lot because ushering brings him or her into close contact with others. Bad breath and body odour could embarrass the members of the congregation, and the usher himself. In effect, people avoid an usher that is careless with personal hygiene.

Love for People

Ushering is all about dealing with people. So, the usher cannot be good and effective without radiating love for people, the type of love that should come from within. It shows in his relationship with people throughout the meeting. The usher should show love naturally and consistently in his dealings with the familiar and the unfamiliar people, the high and the low, and the old and the new members. His inability to radiate love could mar the day for some people—more especially, visitors and young Christians.

Tact and Creativity

This is the art of doing the right thing in the right way at the right time and place without jeopardizing the higher objective. The purpose of ushering is to maintain order at meetings; and this raises a vital question, 'How does the usher ensure order while dealing with someone that is ready to cause disorder at a meeting?' All he needs is tact and creativity. These are indispensable assets in ushering and they show in the way the usher handles situations while getting people comply with his directives. He could get them do things without appearing bossy, without hurting their feelings. Usher's tact could make people enjoy cooperating with him to ensure order at a meeting. Therefore, he must be creative in managing a situation that could easily lead to an ugly scene.

Positive Mental Attitude

Conscious of his calling, an usher maintains the right mindset about the ministry. He works by faith, believing that the Holy Spirit gets things done no matter how daunting they may appear. Situations that try the usher's endurance and patience do arise. Unless he approaches such situations with faith and confidence, he may lose his composure and buckle under pressure. Positive mental attitude means '*I can do all things through Christ*' (Philippians 4:13). The usher does not see problems but solutions; he does not see obstacles but stepping-stones to achieving the Lord's call.

I was virtually on my feet for the three days of the meeting during one of the international conventions of the Full Gospel Business Men's Fellowship International in Lagos. I did not realize the enormity of stress I was going through until the end, at about midnight the third day. I discovered that the inner strength came from my personal conviction that the job must be done and done well, too. I had only asked the Lord for strength and it really came. One of the reasons why people give in to stress in kingdom service is the feeling that they are the ones doing the work.

This attitude takes away the focus from the Lord and puts it on oneself. But one has to be conscious of the presence of the Holy Spirit. In this state, one sees problems and obstacles give way in the face of an all-conquering power of positive mental attitude. Therefore, ushering, more especially, at large meetings is a matter of positive mental attitude as Dr. Sidney N. Bremer states:

> Success in any facet of endeavor is deep-rooted in attitudes, not in aptitudes. The one who holds the positive, hopeful, confident, good-natured, kindly, courageous mental attitude is the person who inevitably radiates sunshine and gladness, good health and cheer, confidence and happiness wherever he may go.[2]

Calm Disposition

The usher should maintain a calm disposition however stormy the situation might be. His personal calmness conveys a sense of peace and assurance to the congregation. It equally shows the inner spiritual strength that arises from faith. Calm disposition enhances creativity and sound judgment.

3
PSYCHOLOGY OF USHERING

The ministry of ushering entails *serving* the *congregation* to ensure *order* in the conduct of a Christian *program*. The key words in this definition highlight the kernel of the ministry:
➢ The *congregation* gathers for a *program*.
➢ The *usher serves* to ensure *order* in its conduct.

Therefore, the quality of usher's service affects the outcome of a program. Its success derives from the ushers' ability to harmonize the roles of all the parties—the principal actors and the congregation.

Like in every normal social relationship, the way we interact with others depends on our understanding of them. This assertion raises two critical questions: how does the individual behave? How does the crowd behave? These questions border on the psychology of human and crowd behavior. So the usher should understand the psychology of both the individual and the crowd to which he ministers. But it does not end there. The spirituality of ushering brings God into the equation. It establishes a tripod that ties God, the congregation, and the usher together. Therefore, the usher needs to know how God sees him, how the congregation sees him, and how he sees himself.

We should look at the following factors that stand out in the psychology of ushering and how they affect ministry effectiveness:
- The crowd behavior.
- The usher as the congregation sees him.
- The usher as he sees himself.
- The usher as God sees him.

CROWD BEHAVIOR

The congregation behaves differently from the individual. It has its own identity and group personality. It follows that when people come together, each person's behavioral traits give way to that of the group. The usher should, therefore, know the factors that influence the nature and form of group behavior, and should be able to put such knowledge to positive use.
- Common background.
- Nature of gathering.
- Social status of the individuals.
- Spiritual maturity of the individuals.
- Ushers effectiveness.

During my time as an usher, I observed that people of

common background (cultural or social), sitting together, would express themselves more freely than if they were from different backgrounds. Consequently, they are noisier and more difficult to handle because of a latent sense of collective solidarity. However, if they sat together as a representative of their church group, they would tend to behave better because of the higher interest of the group they represent.

I also observed that the spiritual or social nature of a gathering influences the behavior of people. For example, at a Christian wedding reception, believers behave differently from the way they would at a purely religious meeting. The purpose of meeting affects the nature of behavior; this equally affects the manner of ushering. Similarly, the social class and maturity level of attendees at a meeting affect their behavior. Thus, ushers have a problem with handling a lower class of people and a teenage group than with a higher class and an adult group. In effect, part of usher's creativity is to know how to adapt to varying situations.

Finally, the style of ushering could affect the behavior of the crowd. If ushers were unfriendly, sloppy, and show signs of ineffectiveness, the crowd could become unmanageable.

What do these observations teach us?

The usher should be able to identify the nature and composition of the group he is ministering to. This type of understanding helps but must couple with good planning in order to achieve an effective ushering.

THE USHER AS OTHERS SEE HIM

Apart from that of the pastor, the ushering ministry puts the Christian worker in the spotlight more than other ministries. The usher typifies the biblical lamp on a hill. He sees everyone in the congregation but does not observe every person. On the contrary, everyone sees and observes him. They observe his dressing, comportment, personality, and the way he attends to people. In the process, they evaluate the usher and form their impressions and expectations. As a 'public relations officer', he reflects the image of the church or Christian organization. In the eye of the congregation, he represents the pastor, and therefore, should know all about the organization and the program. This makes them run to the usher for questions and clarifications concerning the meeting.

THE USHER AS HE SEES HIMSELF

A person's sense of self-worth affects his or her personality. The one that has a bloated self-esteem comports himself in a proud and arrogant manner; this shows in the way he reacts to people and situations. On the other hand, the person with low self-esteem exhibits an inferiority complex; he is withdrawn and unsociable. Each case affects his ministry effectiveness. A biblical illustration of this observation is in the story of the spies that went to Jericho. Ten of the spies saw themselves as grasshoppers, while two saw themselves as mighty men in God's hand (a necessary mindset for working with God).

> *And there we saw the giants, the sons of Anak, which come of the giants: and we were in our own sight as grasshoppers, and so we were in their sight. (Numbers 13:33)*

Undoubtedly, fresh ushers find their first outing before a large audience quite intimidating. However justifiable such a feeling could be, it should not degenerate to an undue consciousness of one's personal limitation. The usher should rather see himself as a person the Holy Spirit equipped to carry out the kingdom work. His confidence should stem from two premises: he works under a divine mandate and that he prepared well for the program.

THE USHER AS GOD SEES HIM

God sees the believer differently in Christ, and if he (the usher) understands his position before God, he should carry out the ministry with confidence. Primarily, God sees the usher not only as His child, but also as a vessel that He uses to achieve His kingdom purpose. Consequently, God fills him with the Holy Spirit and expect him to depend on His power for the ministry. He expects the usher to be Christ-conscious rather than be self-conscious and to work with the primary purpose of glorifying Jesus Christ.

4
PREPARATION FOR USHERING

We have observed, so far, that ushering goes beyond the externals of the ministry. It encompasses the totality of the human person. I have seen enthusiastic workers rush into the ministry, but shortly after they discover that they cannot fit into the mold. They leave in frustration because they missed the biblical 'counting the cost' before enlisting. Therefore, one has to make adequate preparations to effectively apply one's knowledge of psychology of ushering. These are in the areas of:

➢ Physical Preparation.
➢ Mental Preparation.
➢ Social Preparation.
➢ Psychological Preparation.
➢ Spiritual Preparation.

PHYSICAL PREPARATION

The physical demands of ushering arise from long periods of standing, walking around, and answering to people's needs here and there. The usher has to prepare his body to meet these pressures. Part of this preparation is to ensure adequate and balanced feeding to enable the body develop natural resistance to infections. In addition, one should engage in physical exercises to firm up the muscles and raise the general body tone. For example, jogging and indoor stretches to tune up the leg muscles; practice of breath control exercises to firm the lungs, conserve energy, and enhance endurance. It is also necessary to learn the right standing and walking technique-a technique that ensures even distribution of body weight down the whole frame to the legs. This reduces the chances of having back pain. Wrong postures like standing sloppy and with hanging shoulders lead to weakness and sluggishness. In effect, wrong posture is the greatest cause of fatigue, more especially, it is the cause of knee wobbling.

MENTAL PREPARATION

Ushering has a lot to do with anticipation of actions like people's reactions, head usher's instructions, and fellow ushers' moves. Anticipation preempts others' intentions and their next move. This state of alertness keeps the usher on guard most of the time. Mental dullness reflects in poor and ineffective teamwork. The usher should develop interest in understanding human nature and social behavior.

Through such understanding, he gains deeper insight into the principles of the ministry. Part of preparation also involves developing the power of observation; he deals mostly with movements of people. He should be able to observe and interpret the motive behind a person's movement. It also advisable to observe the mature ones minister at meetings, noting how experience interplays with knowledge. Working on one's power of observation, the usher should be able to have a mental picture of the section under his or her control.

In my own experience, I started early in life to develop my power of observation by training to capture objects within my view and registering them in the mind. Then, I would close my eyes and try to capture them as accurately as possible. Coupled with further training on going after details I was able to easily pick the minutest movement around me. This turned to be an asset later. An usher needs to be very sensitive to movements within his area of control.

Again, good food and sound rest play a part. It does not make good sense to keep late night just before the following day's long ministration. Over work and lack of rest dulls the mind. Young ushers tend to overwork themselves, thinking that the sheer strength should be able to carry them on indefinitely.

PSYCHOLOGICAL PREPARATION

A person's mental attitude affects his social relationship. Attitudes derives from one's reaction to life's experiences, and an undue consciousness of these experiences could lead to either inferiority or superiority feelings. None of these is in line with the Christian mindset; they affect the usher's effectiveness.

Psychological preparation should focus on working on one's mindset by dwelling extensively on God's word; the believer needs to agree with what God says he is. Meditating on God's word and affirming what it says about oneself helps to prepare the one psychologically for the ministry.

> ***Nay, in all these things we are more than conquerors through him that loved us. (Romans 8:37)***

Such affirmation is done by deliberately speaking the word of God aloud to oneself, preferably, while standing before a full-size mirror.

SPIRITUAL PREPARATION

Most people see more of the physical and social side of ushering without considering the spiritual aspect. Yet, ushering is more spiritual than it is social. Though the usher moves around in the congregation, he should note that the gathering is a spiritual one. So, he needs the enabling power of the Holy Spirit to minister effectively. He should also remember that Satan has an interest and would like to disorganize the meeting by all means. The usher is a target.

There are two reasons why the usher should prepare spiritually:

- Ushering is a spiritual work that must be done in the power of the Holy Spirit.
- The enemy would mobilize to destabilize the ushering team and destroy the work.

The Scriptures illustrate these spiritual principles and they apply to all aspects of kingdom service.

> *Then he answered and spake unto me, saying, This is the word of the Lord unto Zerubbabel, saying, Not by might, nor by power, but by my spirit, saith the Lord of hosts. (Zechariah 4:6)*

> *For it is God which worketh in you both to will and to do of his good pleasure. (Philippians 2:13)*

> *And they shall fight against thee; but they shall not prevail against thee; for I am with thee, saith the Lord, to deliver thee. (Jeremiah 1:19)*

Spiritual preparation falls on two levels—personal and group—and shows in the quality of ushering at meetings. A spirit-filled ushering team strives to achieve God's purpose and this is where they run into conflict with the enemy (the devil) that has a different purpose for the meeting. Awareness of this conflict of interest should place a sense of responsibility on the usher and the team. Though he functions as an individual, he also functions as a member of a team. Therefore, the purpose of personal spiritual preparation is to enable the usher receive adequate spiritual empowerment for the work and integrate into the team. It also helps him obtain spiritual cover whereby the Holy Spirit shields him from any form of satanic attack.

How does the team prepare spiritually for the ministry? A well-harmonized team functions as one. In a such spiritual unity of purpose, the Holy Spirit operates unhindered and makes it difficult for the enemy to break in. Spiritual preparation both at the individual and corporate levels falls into three main categories:

1. *Fellowship*—good time with the Lord through praise and worship, reading and meditating on the word. This enables the team to flow into His presence and receive cleansing and spiritual enablement.
2. *Prayer*—submitting to God, asking for knowledge, understanding, and wisdom for the work ahead. The team lets God know of its dependence on Him, and obtains confirmation that He is behind the work.
3. *Warfare*—having received assurance of His presence and support, the team rises in faith to exercise the believer's authority over all contending forces of darkness. The battle is won both on the knees, and in prophetic proclamations (Details of usher's spiritual warfare are treated in Chapter 4).

These spiritual disciplines should not be mere rituals but an integral part of the usher's ministry life. Those in ministry need the assistance of the Holy Spirit to do even the slightest aspects of kingdom work, or else, expose themselves to danger. Believers hardly appreciate the spiritual implications of their work in the vineyard until they experience the enemy attack in a physical form. The experience of the sons of Sceva (Acts 19:14) should be a lesson to those that take the devil for granted.

SOCIAL PREPARATION

Teamwork in ushering operates better when members are at peace with themselves and with their colleagues. Essentially, the usher should appreciate that he does not work alone. They need to relate with each other on first name basis, knowing that their effectiveness depends on the extent to which they blend socially. However, freedom of interaction should be within the limits of Christian decency. The ministry has a good representation of young people (young in age and in spiritual life), and should need guidance and direction from the head usher.

PART 2
BUILDING THE TEAM

The use of the expression 'ushering team' calls to mind three terms that explain the secret of success of ushering ministry:
- Team—a group of people that work together to accomplish a particular task.
- Teamwork—the ability of a group of people to work well together.
- Team spirit—willingness to act for the good of one's team rather than for individual personal advantage.

5
EVERY CHURCH NEED A TEAM

As long as there are regular church meetings, an ushering team is an indispensable ministry of the church. This is irrespective of her numerical strength. It is not just enough to call on some dedicated members to carry out ad hoc ushering responsibilities. Though the same purpose could be achieved it does not give character to the organization of the church.

Besides meeting the local needs of the church, an organized ushering ministry helps members understand the value of humility in Christian service, a necessary qualification for leadership position in the church. I observed, in my ushering days, that some members of the congregation regarded ushers as 'servants'. They would speak to them condescendingly and expect them to kowtow in answering to their needs. Though I found this attitude funny, it helped me address the issue of personal pride, which has a negative effect on one's effectiveness in kingdom service.

Having an organized team helps the ushering department to fit into church operational system. It also establishes order and continuity, and gives the ministry its unique identity. While having an administrative structure in place simplifies the daily running of the ministry, there may be a need to set up a temporary operational structure during a major outing. For example, an ushering team that should meet the needs of a large crusade exists to serve the need of the moment. Its structure is entirely different from that of a local church.

A well focused ushering team is a good manpower resource to the church. With the members dedication and commitment, the church could through the team raise pastors and evangelists. The Evangelist Philip's case is a good example. There are many of such cases in modern Pentecostal churches.

Another reason a local church should have an ushering team is to meet the current growing trend in church life worldwide. Networking is fast becoming an essential part of carrying out the Great Commission [World Evangelization]. Thus, largescale crusades, annual conferences, and conventions now involve the collaboration of groups of regional churches. Ushering at such a scale falls outside the responsibility and capability of one church alone. It should involve ushers from participating churches. In such a situation, it would be difficult to provide quality ushering if the ushers themselves had no prior experience in their local churches.

STRUCTURE OF THE MINISTRY

Two or three church members can form the nucleus of an ushering team. The number increases as the church grows in size and expands its operations. A typical ushering team consists of the following:

1. Head Usher—the administrative and spiritual head of the team.
2. Assistant Head Usher—assists the head usher and acts in his place as occasion demands.
3. Secretary—keeps records of meetings along with mailing lists of members, and informs them of the goings-on in the ministry.
4. Treasurer—keeps the purse of the team.
5. Welfare Officer—is responsible for caring for members' social needs.
6. Prayer Secretary—identifies prayer needs and organizes prayer sessions for the team

6
THE HEAD USHER

A group, whether spiritual or secular, must have a leader who should have requisite qualities to direct its operations. However, the qualities of a Christian leader should be above those required for a secular leadership because of the spiritual nature of his position. Thus, the head usher must exhibit the physical, social, and spiritual qualities of a man of God. This consideration should bear on the selection of a head usher, or else a wrong choice could frustrate the ministry and undermine the purpose of the church. With the expanding role of ushering in modern church life, attraction to the office of 'head usher' might becloud its spiritual demands. Thus, wrong persons that seek glamor and honor, but lack the essentials of Christian leadership, can work their way to the top.

In spiritual leadership, external physical appearance of people could be deceptive. Samuel fell prey to this when he went to anoint one of the sons of Jesse as king of Israel. Today, most pastors fall into this same trap while appointing a head usher for the church. Ushering has a lot to do with external appearance and charisma. Unfortunately, these could mask the necessary spiritual conditions for the office and 'deceive' the church into appointing a glamorous, flashy worker into the ushering leadership position. Such leaders have a peacock mentality; they are full of glamor but devoid of effectiveness. They like the public to see them, but have no result to show for the position they occupy. Just as Samuel listened to the Lord, so should the pastor because a person's spiritual qualities do not show on the person's appearance.

QUALITIES OF A HEAD USHER

In selecting a head usher, the pastor should first consider the potential candidate's passion, a noticeable intense desire for the Lord and His work. Without passion, it would be difficult to work with the Lord in the position of a servant. Passion, in this case, does not mean having the right emotional zeal for service; it is rather the spirituality of the zeal that matters most. The second consideration is the person's ability to mobilize and deploy resources—human and material—to achieve the purpose of the church. Peter Wiwcharuck[3] listed the qualities of a Christian leader, which should aptly apply to the head usher.

➢ Integrity—knowing and defending that which is right, even in the face of opposition.

- Honesty—keeping one's activities above reproach before God and man.
- Conviction—this determines the degree of one's dedication to the task God has given.
- Loyalty—to God, to superiors, and to those whom we serve.
- Stability—the ability to accept responsibility and remain true under pressure until the job is done.
- Interest in others—putting the welfare of others ahead of one's own.
- Discernment—gathering all the facts and acting upon them in a conscientious manner.
- Motivation—enthusiasm.
- Tact—showing genuine concern for the feeling of others so as not to cause offence.

RESPONSIBILITIES OF THE HEAD USHER

The responsibility of the head usher is to build an effective ushering team and, at the same time, develop a crop of leaders in their own rights. He should be able to organize, train, motivate, and care for those under his leadership. In effect, his success lies in the ability to identify each member's unique potential and help the one develop and put it to the Lord's use.

The head usher is in-charge of the ushering department whether in the church or in the Christian Fellowship. He receives instructions from, and reports directly to the Pastor or the Chairman of the Planning Committee. In a largescale crusade meeting, he takes charge of the ushering sub-committee. In this capacity, he has a tremendous responsibility of integrating ushering into the operations of the larger group.

Spiritual Leadership

The head usher has spiritual responsibility over members of the team. In effect, he is their 'pastor'; he ministers to their needs, counsels and teaches them, and provides the spiritual cover the ushers need to operate as a team. To succeed in this area, he needs to know members of the team—socially and spiritually—through interaction and intercession. More importantly, he should keep himself spiritually worthy to look after the Lord's flock.

> ***And for their sakes I sanctify myself, that they also might be sanctified through the truth. (John 17:19)***

Recruiting The Ushers

Ushering attracts all types of people because of the seeming social benefits of the ministry. For example, members are popular in the church, are highly visible at meetings, and have easy access to different social groups in the church. Consequently, people who join the ministry on the basis of these 'benefits' cannot contribute meaningfully to the building of an effective team. Ushering needs people that understand the ministry as a divine call. Therefore, the starting point in recruiting members is to pray that God should send in the right workers. Then, one should pray the team into becoming one 'spiritual family.'

Pray ye therefore the Lord of the harvest, that he will send forth labourers into his harvest. (Matthew 9:38)

Young Christians have a problem with identifying their place in kingdom service. They tend to evaluate the work in terms of their personal abilities or such attractive externals of service as we mentioned above. It is better to expose the would-be workers to as many service departments of the church as possible. In the process, each worker identifies the place that suits him or her best.

Organization

He organizes the ushers through regular meetings. In the process, he instils the right team spirit that ensures ministry effectiveness. He identifies different types of talents and gifts, and deploys each person to their areas of strength.

Training

The head usher assesses his team's needs and identifies its training requirements. As he evaluates the impact of training on the general performance of the team, he identifies their individual responses to training. Such members that show creativity in their performance at functions should be groomed for leadership positions. By so doing, he ensures leadership succession in the team.

Motivation

Motivation is a key factor in leadership and vital in the ushering team because of the immense physical and spiritual stress the ushers go through. Regular motivation will help to sustain members' morale. This could come in different forms:

- Always correct the erring ones in love without being bossy. Counselling should go with encouragement.
- Identify with members in social issues that affect members— weddings, birthdays, and bereavements. A personal visit or a card could do a lot of good.
- Appreciate good performance through noticeable actions or open acknowledgement.
- Pray for the individual's needs at ushers' meetings.
- Do not take rash disciplinary action against an erring usher—there might be some emotional or spiritual problems working in the background. The leader needs to go to the Lord in prayer to discover the root of the problem.

When I was president of a Chapter of the Full Gospel Business Men's Fellowship International in Lagos, Nigeria, one of the officers suddenly started behaving uncharacteristically strange. I was peeved; I grumbled and complained, ready to tell him off whenever we met. I was shocked one early morning when, during my quiet time, the Lord asked me if I had prayed for the officer. Indeed, I had not. I had rather been complaining to anyone that was ready to listen. I got the message and started praying for him and he showed up in my house, barely two days later. I wept inside of me as I listened to him recount the terrible experiences he was through since his father died a couple of months earlier. I imagined what further hurt I would have caused him if the Lord had not warned me and I had gone ahead with my plan to confront him.

Motivation can be in the form of taking interest in members' spiritual well being. Some years back, as I was interceding for the members of my team, the Lord revealed that one of them had a serious spiritual problem. I shared the revelation with her. Though not convinced, she went and conferred with a minister outside our local church. There, she had a four-hour deliverance ministration, and the experience she encountered gave her the shock of her life. She came back later, full of appreciation that I went beyond the normal ushering duties to intercede for her. From then, she became more committed than ever. A leader's positive impact on the spiritual lives of the led is a powerful motivational tool in Christian leadership.

The church should take interest in motivating the ushers. In this respect, it may be helpful to encourage a yearly observance of "Ushers' Week." A Sunday service should climax a week-long activity during which the church shows appreciation for their contributions and encourage them for the year ahead.

Finally, the head usher can motivate members by paying special attention to the weak ones, identifying their problems, and helping them get over such.

Creating Team Harmony

An aspect of building a strong ushering team is that of instilling team harmony, which reflects both in spiritual and social relationships. It aims at blending members of the team to function as one. The process of harmonizing offers the ushers the opportunity to smooth down spiritual and social rough edges through corporate prayer and fasting, sharing the word of God together, and ministering to each other's spiritual needs. The Bible says that it takes two to work harmoniously.

Can two walk together, except they be agreed? (Amos 3:3)

Welfare

Timely provision of ushers' ministry requirements is desirable; more especially, such essentials like notebooks, writing materials, and light refreshments can enhance their performance. In addition, large churches that have the means should provide ushers' utility vehicle, and where the campground is away from town, they should provide hostel facilities. The purpose is to alleviate the problems ushers face during an extended program. It is good to provide meals at the end of such protracted ministration.

TIPS FOR THE HEAD USHER

1. Your basic responsibility is to produce the best usher and the best ushering team.
2. Learn the art of managing Christian workers.
3. Lead by example.
4. Make ushering your second nature.
5. Take decisions fast and communicate clearly and promptly.
6. Motivate by rewarding genuine efforts.
7. Express your love and concern for the ushers by surprising them with a card or a visit during birthdays and special occasions.
8. Pray regularly for your ushers. This is the secret of spiritual authority.
9. Never give up on any one. God has a purpose for bringing such one under your spiritual authority.
10. Pray up effectively before the start of functions.
11. Adhere to the secrets of good ushering: effective praying, planning, and supervision.
12. Ensure that things are in place before the function starts. Work ahead of the program.
13. Minister the word of God during the regular departmental meetings.
14. Continue training the ushers until you have trained them. Formulate workable training policy and review it with time.

15. Hold regular praying and fasting meetings.
16. Design enforceable ethics for ushers and ensure compliance.
17. Take interest in the welfare of special guests.
18. Develop a workable system of monitoring and control of offering collections. Keep accurate record of proceedings.
19. Deploy ushers on the basis of their competence.
20. Always watch out for pollutants—glamorous ushers, unsteady characters, sycophants—and weed them out before they damage the team.
21. Prepare for succession.

7
THE TRAINING PROCESS

Life is a continuous learning process. Learning takes place at two levels: learning to know, to acquire a body of knowledge; learning to practice what one has already understood.

People need training and retraining to perform better in any endeavor. The primary purpose of training is to enable a person perform at a good level of behavior and efficiency. While training introduces new ideas and modifies attitudes, retraining reinforces what the person has already learnt and sharpens his or her focus. Training, therefore, enables the ushers to attain such a peak level of performance that ushering becomes a second nature. They respond to situations more out of reflex than of conscious effort. Nobody is an usher by birth; anyone could train to be one. However, some people have the natural behavioral traits for ushering, while others do not. Training can make the difference; the former, to improve on and refine the innate qualities; the latter, to develop new qualities.

The training process should help to identify two basic criteria for eligibility as an usher: the divine call and the personal interest in the ministry. These two factors make training a lot easier, and its effectiveness, measurable. Consequently, training focuses on:
1. Exposing members to basic ushering skills and operations.
2. Enhancing their existing ministerial skills.
3. Enabling them to adjust to changes and developments in the church and society.
4. Imparting teamwork and developing team spirit.
5. Instilling individual and group discipline.

Training can take either a formal or informal form, although the individuals can also augment the training package through self-improvement studies. Whatever the approach, the head usher should not miss the opportunity to impart knowledge and new ideas through correction and counselling as the occasion demands.

FORMAL TRAINING

Formal training involves teaching the theory and practice of ushering. The head usher could organize such training any time and for any duration, depending on the convenience of the trainers and on his assessment of the team's need. This approach is very useful for new entrants because it helps them to come to grips with the fundamentals of ushering. Furthermore, it offers them the opportunity to evaluate their decision to join the ministry. It helps those that cannot fit in to switch to another service department without loss of time.

Formal training could also come in form of a sandwich—the practice of organizing weekend training programmes for those already in the ministry but had no ushering background. The purpose should be to fill up gaps which lack of formal training created and to update the members with recent developments in the ministry.

INFORMAL TRAINING

This is an on-thejob training. It exposes the usher to different aspects of the ministry so that he learns right in the process of actual ushering. In informal training, the head usher or the experienced ones guide the young ushers through the practice of ministering in real life settings. The trainers watch out for mistakes and correct them either in the process or at the end of the meeting.

SELF-IMPROVEMENT STUDY

The usher could undertake to improve his or her ministry through studying appropriate literatures. A diligent, committed usher embarks on general reading of literatures on ushering and puts the knowledge into practice. Also he consciously observes others for better ways of ushering. This mode of learning is commendable because it has self-motivating effect on the individual and helps him or her to sustain a personal interest in the ministry.

TRAINING GUIDELINES

Ushers' training focuses on people, the work, and their relationship with the environment in which they operate. Therefore, the guidelines should reflect the need of the church or the special meeting at which the ushers are to minister. The format should be more comprehensive when dealing with new entrants.

Essentially, training should aim at achieving the following: [3]

1. Advancement of Knowledge.
2. Change of Skill.
3. Change of Attitudes.
4. Change of Behavior.

In order to achieve these results, ushers' training should cover both the Theory and the Practice of Ushering. The purpose is to help the usher to understand the principles of ushering, which enables him or her to minister more effectively. In effect, training succeeds if it makes the individual to know, understand, and do better in the work for which he received training. However, since circumstances and situations are not the same, the following are mere guidelines. They should assist the head usher design a training format more appropriate to the need of his team. It is advisable that training should be as informal as possible and should be within a spiritual setting. Experience shows that spiritual atmosphere should be that of a normal

Christian prayer retreat.

Theory of Ushering
Theory of ushering covers the following segments:

Ushering Environment
1. Exposing members to basic ushering skills and operations.
2. Enhancing their existing ministerial skills.
3. Enabling them to adjust to developments and changes in the church and society.
4. Imparting teamwork and developing team spirit.
5. Instilling individual and group discipline.

The Usher and The Work
1. Assessment of Usher's Potential.
2. The Usher and the Team
3. Secrets of Success in Teamwork
4. Communication Skills for Ushers

Understanding Human Behavior
1. The Behavior of the Individual
2. Group Behavior
3. Factors that Influence Behavior

The Practice of Ushering

This segment focuses on the practical side of the ministry. It involves demonstrating and rehearsing all aspects of the theory until the trainees have known them. Demonstrations should be as near to real life as possible. It should communicate the basic principles of receiving and seating guests, offering collection, handling abnormal cases of behavior, handling an emergency, and general ministrations. It might help to involve members in appraising each demonstration, and thereby make the training experience a participatory one. In the course of this, the ushers watch out to see the theory lessons reflect in the practical demonstrations. For example, comportment, carriage, cheerfulness, and poise are all demonstrable aspects of ushering that the usher should be able to observe during the practical side of training.

PART 3
USHERING IN ACTION

"Ballet dancers practice technique. Pianists wear down their black and white keys with hours of daily practice. Actors rehearse, and rehearse again. Painters perfect still-life objects at various angles, and practice obtaining the best perspectives, experiment with color and texture, do sketches in preparation for oil. By practice one learns to use what one has understood."[4]

The above excerpt from Sol Stein's book, *Solutions for Writers*, summarizes the ushering ministry. The usher needs training to grasp the principles of the art. But he needs practice to "learn to use what he has understood." The preceding chapter is all about training. The following three chapters focus on another form of training: learning to use what the usher has understood.

8
GENERAL PRINCIPLES

We discover the secrets of ushering as we study and meditate on God's word. Being part of the operations of the Godhead, ushering shows in the acts of God, Christ, and the Holy Spirit.

GOD IN CREATION

Before He created the universe, God had a complete blueprint of what He wanted to achieve. In other words, He had the total picture in view. He started with each component unit, took each a day at a time, and put all in place before creating man. In other words, man came into the picture after God had already established an order on earth. By implication, before God allows a spiritual program to go ahead, He has already established the necessary spiritual order for its success. The duty of an usher is to tap from the spiritual resources available.

CHRIST IN OPERATION

In relative terms, a crowd of 5000 at the time of Jesus could compare favourably with a gathering of over a million people in our time. Similarly, the availability of a paltry five loaves of bread and two fishes should have caused panic scrambling in our modern quick-grab culture. Yet the Lord managed the situation well. Why? He knew that, in spiritual arithmetic, a crowd is a collection of individuals. The divine principle is that God sees the individual instead of the crowd—He can make individuals out of a crowd and a crowd out of individuals. Consequently, Christ grouped the 5000 crowd into humanly manageable numbers of 50s and 100s. Then, He multiplied the units of bread and fish to meet the need of the individual.

HOLY SPIRIT IN MANIFESTATION

One hundred and twenty men were praying in a room when the Holy Spirit came on them with strange manifestation—speaking in unknown tongues. This attracted a large crowd of people, a mixed crowd of scoffers and curious onlookers. Knowing the disdain with which the people held the story about Jesus Christ, one would have expected a rowdy reaction against the strange happening. Yet, there was calm as Apostle Peter addressed the bewildered crowd, an address that caused about three thousand people to accept Jesus as Lord and Savior.

"Those who believed what Peter said were baptized

and added to the church—about three thousand in all." (Acts 2:41 NLT)

The presence of the Holy Spirit was evident in keeping the crowd under control, or else, an unwelcome development would have vindicated the scoffer's allegation of drunkenness.

The apostle Peter must have applied the Lord's principle in baptizing such a number of new converts. If all the 120 disciples were directly involved in the immersion baptism that took place, it means that each baptized about 25 persons—another example of reducing a crowd to manageable numbers.

How do these illustrations relate to ushering?

When God approves of a gathering for the furtherance of the kingdom purpose, He first establishes the spiritual atmosphere for order and good conduct. The duty of the ushering team, then, is to hook on to God's order and impose it on the gathering. They accomplish this through prayer and fasting and by complementing the spiritual provision with effective planning and preparation to ensure that necessary requirements—man, materials, seating, and general traffic flow—are in place. This is the only way to keep a gathering under control, in spite of its size.

Though the apostles were waiting for the promise of the Father (Acts 1:3-8) they did not anticipate the events that followed the outpouring of Holy Ghost power. In other words, though they did not plan for the happenings at

Pentecost, they met the challenge and held the situation under control. When the ushering team has prayed and planned effectively for a meeting, the Holy Spirit takes care of the success of events, containing the effects of negative spirits, and causing peace to reign. The spiritual principle is that divine power flows to where the will of God reigns. So whoever works in furtherance of His will receives divine support—this is the secret of ushers' success.

The focus of this book is on ushering at two levels: the local church meetings and interdenominational largescale meetings—crusades and annual local church conventions. It is, therefore, necessary to establish the structure of each level at which the usher ministers before we discuss the nature of planning that should follow. However, the principles of ushering at both levels are the same but the scales of planning and execution differ.

9
THE LOCAL CHURCH

The local church is a physical corporate expression of a spiritual body—the Body of Christ. It has a personality, an image, and a goal. The ushering team, as part of this body, identifies with its goals and functions to achieve its eternal essence.

The physical church is under the human leadership of the pastor who, through the advice of its leadership structure, pilots its affairs. It operates through series of organized functions—mostly on regular basis, and in some cases, ad hoc. The essence of these functions is to bring souls into God's kingdom and teach and nurture them to spiritual maturity. Therefore, ushering, as part of ministry of helps, assists the pastor to achieve these noble divine goals. The usher exists within the church and operates within its structured life.

It is worth mentioning that the church does not belong

to any particular member, but to Jesus Christ, the living founder and head. He established the church with the purpose of saving souls from the power of darkness—World Evangelization. He empowered the church to keep and nurture these souls until His Second Coming (Acts 2:47). Thus, He assigns specific roles to members within specific ministries of the church. Each person's role and ministry complements those of others. This explanation is necessary to enable the usher appreciate that his ministry has a place in God's plan.

The usher is a helping hand, an imagemaker, and a crisis manager—all rolled in one. Consequently, the scope of ushering has gone beyond the traditional roles of greeting and seating people in the church. It follows that they have to keep abreast of societal and global changes; they need to update themselves if they were to remain relevant to their calling. For example, the average life expectancy is changing the world over, with about 75 and 50 in most developed and developing societies respectively. The implication is that there will be a good number of elderly people in the former and young people in the latter. This raises practical questions: How does the usher cope with the problem of catering for the two extremes? How does he assist the elderly in a wheel chair where the physical planning of the church environment does not provide for the mobility of the handicapped? How does he use the seating arrangement to accommodate the growing needs of the elderly? How does he contain the restiveness and excesses of the young? There is no doubt that these limitations would create more work for the usher.

In real terms, ushering deals with people, materials, the physical environment, and time, how to manage them to achieve the goals of the local church or Christian organization. Among all the factors in the equation, the physical environment is a constant, while every other thing is a variable.

Ushering at the local church is not as simple as it appears to be. Many ushers may hold this simplistic view because of their familiarity with the ushering environment, members of the congregation, the pattern of service, and the regular program. Consequently, they overlook the demands of ministry and relapse into a false feeling of complacency. In no time, ushering gradually loses its creativity and excitement, its necessary spiritual punch and fervor.

PLANNING TO USHER

A Christian gathering is spiritual project that aims at glorifying and achieving God's purpose. So, He is interested and, consequently, operates in a small gathering as He would in a large one. He does this by sending the Holy Spirit, knowing that the enemy would attempt at disorganizing the meeting. What is the implication of this observation? Ushers should not allow the size of a meeting to influence their individual and corporate preparedness for ministration.

A biblical example will illustrate this point.

Joshua prepared adequately for his military campaign against the city of Jericho and in the process, God revealed the victory strategy; the well-fortified city wall come down without Joshua's firing a shot. In the glow of that victory, he took the victory over the tiny nation of Ai for granted and glossed over effective planning and seeking the face of God. The outcome proved an embarrassing disaster because, unknown to Joshua, there was a gap in his spiritual armor, a gap that God would have revealed if he had spiritually prepared well.

The purpose of planning for a regular and normal church service meeting is to avert Joshua's experience. Essentially, planning addresses issues like workforce and materials requirements, and the deployment of the same for the success of a meeting. It also takes care of the spiritual aspect of the meeting. Planning for the church service should take place not later than a day before the meeting and should take care of the following key issues:

1. Review of performance at the previous service session with a view to correcting observed errors and lapses.
2. Preview of the following day's service. The head usher should know what special events to expect at the day's meeting, for example, special thanksgiving, child dedication, and such nonregular events that would require ushers' special attention.

3. Distribution of functions to individual ushers. Assigning functions just at the beginning of service session smacks of inadequate planning and lack of understanding of ushering. A better plan is to design a monthly duty roster, where ushers know their positions and roles for each meeting within the period. The practice instils discipline and eliminates the tendency for some to minister at preferred areas.
4. Study of the following day's Sunday school lessons. This would help them to concentrate on ministering during the normal session.
5. Short exhortation given by the person that was appointed earlier for that purpose. Prayers for the members and for the meeting should come at the end of the exhortation.

USHERING AT THE CHURCH SERVICE

Ushering starts well before the main service. The team has to arrive early, prepare the seats, get materials ready, and position themselves according to the duty roster. Equally, ushers leave the church late. They have to ensure that they secure left personal items, enter appropriate records of the day's meeting, and tidy up the place of worship for another program, if any.

Keeping the worship environment neat and tidy may be the responsibility of another group but the ushers should ensure that the worship setting reflects the image of the church. This may involve helping those in charge of decorations to get things right. It could also mean ensuring the conveniences are well kept. The ushers' interest in these areas may be misunderstood as an intrusion. But they should do it out of the concern for the corporate image of the church, which they stand to project.

Details of ushering during church service and the control of the parking lot are treated in later chapters. However, two critical issues peculiar to church service need mentioning.

Handling Offering Collection

This sensitive part of ushering deals with money. Ushers are responsible for the physical cash and bank checks right from collection to entry in the record books. At this point, a duly appointed member of the church leadership takes over the monies, after authenticating the entries. The head usher has no business taking the collection home or even to the bank.

It is advisable to put in place some controls to protect the ushers' integrity. This is necessary because the devil can easily stir up the suspicion of their tampering with the cash collections. During my days as head usher, my pastor once approached me with a courteous advice to "mind my ushers." That advice kept me thinking for a time until I found out that news had gone round that the ushers were helping themselves from Sunday collections. A few days later, the pastor discovered that a staff (not an usher) in the church office had actually gone to cash a check meant for the church. It would have been embarrassing if I had not set up an effective control for handling monies. While we trust each other, we should assist each other by reducing the members' chances of falling into temptation. It is, therefore, preferable to have matured and gainfully employed ushers to take charge of offering monies. But this should be rotational to avoid an usher staying longer than necessary in that beat. Similarly, I do not advise a couple should be in the same group of ushers handling church collections at any time.

Entries should indicate the different denominations of cash and also details of bank checks. There should be different entries for offering, tithe, and special thanksgiving offering. Usually, the head usher should endorse the entry before handing over to the church authority.

Handling Special Members

The design of most of older church buildings did not provide access for the elderly and those on wheel chair. Modern designs do. The usher can only provide limited assistance in the former, but in the latter, he has to assist such people right from the entrance to a convenient seating location, preferably, near an exit. Seating them near an exit ensures a hitch-free evacuation in time of emergency. But this poses a problem as such people would like to stay close to relations and friends. Thus, the order of seating people has to accommodate this peculiar need.

On handling the elderly, an excerpt from Pastor Buddy Bell's book will be of immense help:

> Offer your arm to assist elderly people to their seat. If they prefer to walk on their own, walk slowly to the accessible seat you've chosen for them. Don't show any impatience or irritation. If they take your arm, tell them how far you are going as you walk slowly. Ask them if they have any special needs or might need assistance to the restroom. Above all, always treat the elderly with respect." [5]

The summary of Pastor Bell's suggestion is that the usher should be sensitive to the elderly. The same principle applies to the handicapped.

In effect, ushering at the local church is more sensitive than at a nondenominational large gathering. Reasons for this are many. The church would like to send across the right message to both the traditional members and to new comers. People would like to know how organized and focused a church is, the nature of the environment, and the social class of members. The old view that it does not matter as long as there is love among members and that God's word is the rule of conduct does not hold any longer. The society to which the modern church ministers to has attained a high lifestyle. This reflects in both the home and office environment. It is foolhardy to presume that this does not affect people in their choice of a local church.

So, special members are not only those on wheel chair. Ushers should see every comer as a special member. When I first attended the King's Church Cleethorpes in the north of England, the ushers at the entrance accorded me a "royal" reception. I felt at home right from the door, forgot my "blackness" in a white environment, and enjoyed the fellowship of the Body of Christ. The instant message was, "This is a loving church." Consequently, I got integrated in the church life throughout my stay and the leadership took interest in the purpose of my being in the UK. At the heart of everyone is the desire to be a queen or a king in their own rights. Ushers can make people realize this desire, even for a brief moment.

A socially well-placed Christian woman, in search of a new place of worship, attended a church in Lagos. Dressed in a way that belied her class, she was surprised to see the ushers all over the place, clownishly welcoming the people of substance they knew. A few Sundays after, she decided to attend service in one of the best cars in the family collection. On arrival, the ushers tripped on each other struggling to play the chaperon. She took time off to lecture them on the meaning of Christian love in the ministry of ushering. What could have happened if the woman had not made up her mind to stay in that church?

10
LARGE-SCALE MEETINGS

A growing trend in church life worldwide points towards groups of churches or para-church organizations coming together to host largescale crusades, annual conventions, and conferences. Unlike the local church, a largescale meeting addresses a specific purpose and lasts for a short duration. The participating groups contribute members to the planning committee (Crusade Planning Committee [CPC]), which is under a chairperson. The CPC, after establishing the nature and scope of the function, sets up technical sub-committees, which equally draw membership from the groups. As the name implies, each sub-committee is responsible for detailed planning of the segment of the meeting within its own area of competence. A sub-committee has a chairperson, who is part of the main planning committee. The ushering team comes under such subcommittees.

At this level of function, ushering goes beyond the capacity of one particular group. Ushers from the participating groups come together and build up a team that should meet the purpose of the meeting. Many issues are involved: the work force and materials requirements, venue, duration of meeting, size of audience, and other incidental factors. The way to get around addressing these issues is to start the planning meetings early, bearing in mind that there might be no reliable planning data.

PLANNING TO USHER

The head usher, being a member of the main committee and also the head of the ushering technical sub-committee, understands the scope of his team's involvement and how their role dovetails with those of other sub-committees. Planning, therefore, ensures a seamless integration of ushering with the work of other subgroups. The early stages of meetings should focus on team building, training, socializing, and creating spiritual environment that is conducive to harmonious teamwork. In the process, potential leaders would emerge, and such leaders would take charge of smaller groupings during actual ministrations. I discovered, from personal experience, that one can harmonize a spiritual group through series of prayer and training sessions. As the meetings progress, the Lord would drop those that do not fit into the occasion.

Planning meetings should cover the following major issues:

1. Evaluate the work force and materials requirements.
2. Identify likely problems and proffer solutions to them.
3. Define and assign responsibilities and establish targets.
4. Appraise and evaluate the progress at every stage of preparation.
5. Create spiritual awareness and infuse team spirit.
6. Sharpen individual and corporate focus on the function.
7. Update members on major policy changes at the main committee level.

Work force and Materials Requirements

Many factors determine planning for the work force and materials requirements. These include, number of attendees, nature and duration of the meeting and its timing. While it is possible to ascertain the nature and duration of a meeting, the volume of attendance depends on many internal and external factors. Such issues like theme of the meeting, caliber of ministers, quality of publicity, and possibility of other functions holding at the same time affect the public's response to the meeting. In developing societies, an unpredictable social and political environment could affect the turnout at a meeting. Thus, the absence of reliable planning information makes it difficult to assemble and train the right number of ushers. Besides, one should note that the number of interested ushers always starts high but thins down as the training progresses. This, again, reduces the margin of certainty in the ability of the team to cope with an unknown volume of work.

What does the head usher do?

He has to establish a worst-case scenario and plan toward it. Experience shows that it is better to provide in excess than to run short of men, a situation that could throw the ushers into confusion and force the head usher to engage non-ushers. After establishing a tentative working number, the head usher should apply the Lord's principle by assigning a mature usher to supervise the work of a group of ushers, each of whom ministers to a seating of about 250 attendees or more. This approach lightens the work, makes for easy communication among the ushers, and relieves the head usher of needless stress. Where possible, it is good to have enough hands to take charge of smaller segments of congregation.

Planning for materials requirements—offering bags, decision cards, ushers' identification badges, record books, and printed notices—works out better toward the start of the meeting than at the early stages of preparation because a clearer picture emerges as the time approaches. This does not, however, apply to the provision of such essentials that are useable beyond the present meeting. Nevertheless, procurement of materials should start in good time, to avoid anxiety and confusion normally associated with their late arrival.

Identifying Likely Problems

Planning entails making a comprehensive appraisal of issues that could affect the running of the meeting. Through projections and deductions the ushering team should be able to proffer likely solutions and take preemptive actions. It will be sheer naivety to ignore the unexpected and assume that everything would work hitch-free. The head usher, being part of the CPC, updates his team with changes at the higher level. This enables them to adjust their own planning accordingly.

I learnt from experience that inadequate work force is a usual problem that surfaces at an awkward time, when the meeting is in progress. The head usher discovers suddenly that attendance has far outstripped the planned figure. Panic sets in as failure stares him in the face. What does he do? Initial mistake is to rush around mobilizing every available willing hand. This is a gross spiritual error because it offers the enemy an opportunity to infiltrate the team. The head usher should do nothing in the circumstance. There is no fire brigade approach to ushering. He should just allow *"the great storm to become a great calm"* (Mark 4:39). But his ability to take such a development in its strides depends on whether he anticipated and prepared for it during the planning stage, whether he had trained the ushers for endurance and stability under pressure. In other words, there is a need to make contingency plans for the unexpected, bearing in mind that pressure is part of ushering at large meetings.

Defining and Assigning Tasks

All members of the ushering team take part in the planning. This enables them to have a true feel of the function and work to achieve its success. At the planning meeting, the ushers look for the areas of the function that fall within their control. Then, they identify the things that need attention, assign relevant tasks to members, and set targets for achieving them. Subsequent meetings provide the chance to assess the progress at each stage and take extra measures where necessary.

Creating Spiritual Awareness

The regular prayer and fast that go with planning meetings help create the right spiritual atmosphere for the outing. It instils team spirit in members and sharpens their spiritual focus on the function.

Venue Preparation

There are two types of venues: a purposebuilt public meeting place like the stadium, town hall, and a conference centre; an open field, which the organizers plan to meet the desired layout. Our discussion on venue preparation focuses on the latter.

Preparing the venue of a meeting means that the organizers should take both spiritual and physical control over it. Spiritual control takes the form of occasional prayer visits during which, the ushers march around, dedicating the venue to the Lord, commanding the environment to submit to the authority of the Lord Jesus Christ. This is irrespective of similar outings by the Prayer and Fasting Sub-Committee. A serious spiritual battle, it entails displacing any form of spiritual territorial controls, the negative forces that would hinder the meeting.

To take physical control, the ushers first, study the venue. If it is a purposebuilt place, they should identify the locations of existing facilities that will serve the purpose of the meeting. In the case of an open field, the heads of Ushering and Facilities Sub-Committees have to establish the right locations for activities. In either case, they should mark out spaces for the following: Altar, Seating, Ministers' Rest Room, Counselling Room, Audio Visual Room, Emergency Exits, First Aid Room, Toilets, Information Desk, Tapes and Books Sales Corner, Food and Refreshments Corner, Security Post, Lighting Control Points, and Water Hydrants. If, however, the venue is an open field, the ushers have to propose the right locations to site the facilities. Finally, they should harmonize traffic flow into the venue with that of the surrounding, such that major aisles, defined with seating arrangements, can connect effectively with main entrance points.

Defining The Traffic Flow

The principle of traffic planning derives from the fact that people flow to where there are activities, and in large scale meetings, successful planning shows in the people's ability to interact with minimal discomfort and distraction. Some activities take place within the main arena, while others without; the traffic flow should incorporate the two by the use of aisles.

The width of an aisle depends on the volume of human traffic it carries. Primary aisles radiate from the Altar and lead straight to both the entry points and the Counselling Room. The secondary aisles feed the primary ones and serve to break the overall seating arrangement into manageable portions. This approach makes movement easy and enhances ushering. It also reduces the whole seating arrangement to the human scale, making it easy for the people to locate their position in the congregation. It is advisable to organize the seating in multiples of 100s as a good way of easing the job of collecting offering, taking the head count, distributing literature materials, and ensuring an effective monitoring of the congregation.

The Altar

The altar is the most important part of the venue. Being the main focus in the arena because of the nature of activities that take place there, ushers should restrict the frequency and volume of movement toward it. The altar area could be rowdy during deliverance ministration and praying for individuals. There could be a noticeable move of the Holy Spirit, when many fall under the power of anointing. If adequate clearance is not provided, the situation could be unmanageable. It is, therefore, necessary to provide enough floor space of about 5 metres (15 feet) between the altar and the first row of seats.

USHERING DURING MEETINGS

In spite of elaborate meeting planning, the real test of ushering comes during the meeting, a time when theory is put into practice. The test, which is spiritual, physical, and emotional, reveals the usher's competence, preparedness, and fitness for the ministry.

The Program

The program guides all the parties to the function and helps the ushers to understand and fit into the flow of the meeting. They should study the program before the commencement of the function. This enables them to stay ahead of events and prepare for any alterations that might come up along the way. Most times, lack of understanding of the program leads to the inability to follow along and, therefore, contributes to ineffective and sloppy ushering. Ushers should know that the whole meeting revolves around the program and its mode of implementation defines the mood and outcome of the meeting.

At the FGBMFI Lagos Conventions of 1996 and 1999, the ushers would be set ahead of an event in the program by about five minutes. Hence, they did not react to an announcement of an event but were rather ready for it to take off. For example, ushers would be ready with the offering bags even before the call was made. It applied throughout different segments of the meeting and proved valuable in time management. In effect, a good understanding of the program keeps the ushers relaxed.

Manning and Teamwork

The usher has to be spiritually alert to take charge of his segment of the congregation effectively. Spiritual alertness means being sensitive to the leading of the Holy Spirit and thereby stay ahead of the enemy. He does this by being conscious of the fact that he is working under the authority of the Holy Spirit and by staying at a strategic point from where he could visually cover his section. It is advisable to sit, preferably, at the aisle end of the last row of the section. From such a vantage point, he could visually scan the section once in a while. Thus, it becomes unnecessary to walk up and down the aisle without a justifiable reason.

Ushers do not work alone but as a team. This means that while each controls a portion of the congregation, he has to maintain contact with others and also with his supervisor. He does not achieve this by walking around to whisper to other ushers, but through regular eye contact. With this, he avoids causing unnecessary distractions.

Welcoming Guests

Ushering starts at the entrance; and guests get a feel of the meeting from the way ushers receive them on arrival. We observed earlier that the usher is the window through which a guest sees the organization. Therefore, an amiable atmosphere at the entrance should saturate the whole ushering environment all through. In welcoming guests, the usher should follow the ushering ministerial ethics:

radiate an infectious cheerfulness, avoid hugging and embracing (this disrupts free flow of traffic; it could also embarrass some guests), look people straight in the eye while exchanging pleasantries. While we freely express Christian love toward others, we should know when such acts cause offence. In this wise, the usher should respect the other person's personal space by not coming too close for comfort, more especially while dealing with the opposite sex or a complete stranger.

Receiving Special Guests

Courtesy demands that ushers should accord the special guests their due respect and honour. This also applies to highly placed people, whether they are special guests or not. The head usher should take special interest in receiving such guests, and if possible, walk them to their seats. In some cases, seats are reserved for special guests, and such seats remain reserved until it becomes necessary to fill them. At times, a special guest comes so late that taking him to the high table could be distracting. What does the head usher do? I believe that ushering allows room for discretion. He should know when to consult with the program coordinator.

Occasionally, a needless misunderstanding arises between the ushers and protocol officers regarding leading special guests to the high table. The head usher is responsible for controlling movements during the meeting. Viewed from this definition, the protocol officer should hand over special guests to the head usher.

Seating The Congregation

Rules that guide the seating of members of congregation as they come into the meeting derive from the purpose of ushering, which is to maintain order with minimal distraction. With this in mind and by applying simple ushering rules, high standard of ushering could result at a meeting.

1. Seating should start from the first row of a section and flow toward the back row. However, allow preferred seating for early arrivals if they so desire.
2. In a row with aisles on both sides, seating should start from the centre toward the ends. If, however, the row abuts a wall, seating should begin from the wall end to the aisle.
3. As much as possible, allow families or people that come together to sit close, except where children should be in their section. However, genuine personal reasons could make the usher allow children sit with their parents.
4. Lead people to their seats, and not let them roam about.
5. Where it is not possible to walk a guest to a seat, it is better to hand him to the nearest usher, who should hand him to the next usher until he is seated.
6. Watch out for unwanted personal items like umbrellas, walking sticks, and any thing that could

cause obstruction to free movement. Politely collect such from the owner and keep the same in a safe place until the end of the meeting.

Distributing Items

Items like fliers, literature materials, and pledge forms are usually distributed at meetings. Ushers assemble such items well ahead of time and arrange them for easy distribution within their sections. A good way to ensure smooth operation is to package and distribute them according to rows and down the aisle.

Offering Collection

Offering collection poses one of the greatest problems at large functions. Incidentally, this is an item that attracts much attention from the organizers of the program. Offering is a sensitive issue to the planning committee, who would like to recover as much of the cost as possible, or, if possible, have an excess to use for future meetings. The congregation is interested, too. So, all eyes are on the ushers. The head usher should work out the best approach to meeting these expectations.

Three basic issues are involved in collecting offering: speed, efficiency, and transparency.

Speed

Some factors determine the speed of collection: the number of both ushers and offering bags available, the level of usher's preparedness before the start of offering, the manner in which ushers gave out the offering bags, and the ease with which the bags flow along the rows. It is time wasting for the head usher or his supervising ushers to walk about giving out offering bags to the ushers just at the very start of collection. The bags should be ready well ahead of time. Equally, offering should follow the order of seating, and flow from the front to the back row. Collection is faster when people see those in front put in their offering; they get prepared before the bag gets to their turn. Collecting from the rear takes many unawares. Finally, the usher should watch over the flow of offering bag; he should politely motion a faster flow if there were a bottleneck down the row.

Effectiveness

This is a measure of percentage coverage of offering collection, which largely depends on the same factors that affect the speed of collection. With insufficient ushers and bags, it will be difficult to reach a good number of the congregation. Even if the bags were in good supply, poor coverage could arise from the ushers not giving them out in time and, for lack of time, the bags cannot go round. I observed that the nature of seating arrangement affects the quality of collection. In most open meetings in Nigeria, attendance usually outstrips the seating provisions. In such situations, it becomes impossible to reach a good number of attendees because of the crowd around the meeting. However, even if the bags manage to reach the deep recesses of the crowd, one cannot guarantee the safety of the collections. A situation like this developed some years back, during which a group of 'volunteer ushers' smiled home with both the offering bags and the collections.

The relationship between the total collection and total attendance gives a good indication of the effectiveness of collection. A quick check could throw some light: a gathering of about 5000 adult participants giving an offering of ₦1.0 each should amount to ₦5000.00. A collection that is grossly under this figure should cast doubt on the quality of collection.

Transparency

Members of the church or the organizing group have interest in the offering collection; at least, their eyes follow the movement of the ushers and the collection bags. My personal principle is to ensure that people can observe what I am doing during the collection process. Consequently, the following guidelines could enhance transparency:

1. Ensure that the bags are deep enough to reduce the chances of one reaching deep down into it during collection?
2. Raise the bags conspicuously when passing them down the rows and when in the ushers' possession.
3. Discontinue with the collection and safeguard the bags if, for any reason, the collection has to stop abruptly.
4. Count the monies in a safe place, away from the general public, and make the entries in appropri-

ate forms (in multiples). Ensure that the right persons sign the completed forms. In most largescale meetings, members of the Finance Sub-Committee observe the counting and endorse the entries.
5. Where there are multiple collections at a function, the head usher should assign a different team to count and record each collection.

HEAD COUNT

The purpose of head count is to record the level of attendance at a meeting and provide planning statistics for future meetings. It is not easy to obtain exact figures at large meetings, but approximate number is good enough for the purpose. However, right timing for a head count is necessary to obtain a fair figure, and the head usher should apply his experience to identify the right moment.

Arranging seats in sectors and in predetermined multiples of, say, 100s simplify the head count. The usher needs to count the number of vacant seats and subtract it from the total number within his sector. Counting the large congregation in sectors reduces the margin of error.

SPECIAL MINISTRATION

Special ministration comes up when, for instance, the speaker invites people with special needs to come to the altar for prayers. In effect, many people come to the program for 'special' prayers. Two things are likely to happen as a result of this call:

1. The congregation surges forward and congests the aisles and altar area.
2. Some people may fall under the power of the Holy Spirit, thereby creating rowdy atmosphere around the altar.

However, the possibility of these things happening depends largely on the type and class of preacher—his popularity, charisma, and style of ministration. Thus, the ushers should prepare accordingly for such occasions.

Therefore, it is advisable to take the sectors in turn and channel traffic down the primary aisles and, then, arrange the people in a row before the altar to enable the ministers pray for them in an orderly manner. Some of the people could fall under the power of the Holy Spirit. So an usher should stand behind to break the person's fall, but the usher should neither stand behind an opposite sex nor break the fall of a person heavier than he is. If someone turns violent, a group of ushers should rally round to restrain the person and take him or her to the counselling room, if necessary. No matter the pressure, it is not advisable to involve non-ushers to minister in such a situation.

HANDLING EMERGENCY

An emergency situation could arise from causes outside anybody's control or making. Such a development, normally referred to as Act of God, could be fire outbreak, rain storm and wind effect on big tents during outdoor meetings, and power outage. At times, some devilish hoodlums could create a situation. Whichever one throws the congregation into a panic and leads to a stampede.

Emergency tests the ushers' ability to remain calm and allay fears in the congregation in a panic situation. In managing such occasions, the head usher should apply a first line emergency control measures' he should speedily identify the likely cause of panic and determine how to guide the congregation out of danger. It may be necessary to use the public address system to allay fears and stem stampede, while ushers take over strategic locations and control the congregation effectively.

Although emergency is not a regular feature, a wise precaution is to plan for it, failing which could result in unwelcome consequences. In effect, part of the familiarization visits is to identify the locations of such emergency control features as fire extinguishers, water hydrants, and power control points. The aisles should be clear of obstacles like chairs, protruding pews, and personal effects. In addition to planning, the ushers should train their eyes for suspicious movements and alert the head of security promptly.

RECORD KEEPING

Record keeping is an important aspect of ushering; the day's ministration is not complete without adequate records of statistics of the meeting. Records give a quick assessment of the meeting and provide planning data for the future. At the local church worship services, records help the pastor appreciate the general health statistics of the church. Records cover areas like decisions, collections, attendance, and other special information that may be peculiar to a meeting. In effect, records should be as exhaustive as possible. The usher should crosscheck all the figures before entering them in the forms. There should be record of unused items like literature materials. These forms are filled in multiples and duly signed. Lost and found items are recorded and tagged to help identify the rightful owners.

Finally, record keeping imparts discipline and accountability on the team. It makes for transparency and attracts the trust of church leadership. Therefore, the head usher should take this seriously and train every member of the team in the discipline of keeping accurate records.

11
USHERING AT THE CAR PARK

We live in an age of cars; owning one is no longer a luxury. It is a necessity, the type many would like to do away with, if possible, because of the problems that go with it. The trouble with the motor car is that it has become such a part of modern culture that the planning of cities and life within them revolve around the use of cars. Hence the planning authorities impose strict guidelines on the design of public spaces like churches and other places of worship or large gatherings because of the volume of car traffic such facilities attract. Therefore, there has to be good provision of space and security for car parking.

So, managing the car park, both at the local church level and at large gatherings, is a factor in modern ushering. It places a lot of strain on the team, more so, when there is not enough workforce to handle such an added function.

The work of ushering at the car park has a lot of implications; it demands more than the usher is naturally trained for. For example, the control of vehicular traffic is the work of trained city officials; keeping an eye on likely car thieves is the work of the police and trained security operatives, those licensed to carry firearms. If the situation dictates, the ushers should involve, from outside the church, persons who trained in these special areas. However, the head usher should deploy a person with driving skill to head the team in charge of the car park.

In the light of the above, the ushers should consider the follow key issues in planning for the car park during functions:
- Security
- Space management
- Traffic flow

SECURITY

Security covers protection for the usher and the cars. Ushers should protect themselves from reckless drivers and from hoodlums who come to steal. Security for the cars depends on the nature of the parking lot. There is more exposure to risk in an open field parking than in an enclosed parking. The situation differs in developing countries, where a street urchin does not need to steal a car but the fittings (headlamps, pointers, and external car accessories) that can give him easy cash for a punch or a pot.

In societies that are prone to violence, the ushers should wear protective gadgets like bulletproof vests. They should also have the communication facilities to alert the police in the event of violence. The use of cell phones, pagers, and walkietalkie sets could enhance their ability to make the necessary contacts and get timely help.

It is good to work out effective, manageable control measures in handling cars, starting from the point of entry until all cars exit the lot. But first, the ushers should designate separate parking areas for the ministers and special guests, duty vehicles, and the people who indicate to leave the venue before the end of meeting. It is equally a good idea to issue number tags at the point of entry and collect them at the point of exit. In an extensive open parking without a surrounding fence, ushers should position themselves at strategic locations, from where they can monitor movements within the parking lot. They should put on reflexive vests to stand out from a distance. In overnight meetings, it is advisable to install closecircuit television gadgets to have a good watch over vehicles and movements within the parking lot. There should be good lighting.

Depending on the nature and scope of function, the presence of armed security personnel can deter intending car thieves. Their presence should be seen. So, it is worth the while applying for such assistance from the local police. All these preparations and precautions work out fine if attendees park within the parking lot.

During one of the conventions in Lagos, members of the Convention Planning Committee had an all night planning and prayer meeting. Cars were parked outside because of lack of space within the premises; this attracted the attention of robbers at the early hours of the morning. Although no lives were lost, the experience was traumatic. However, such an incident is not peculiar to parking outside an enclosed area. It once happened in my local church, during a Sunday morning service. I was literally shattered when I heard, at the end of service, that a brand new car was missing. The woman owner was hysterical; a feeling of guilt and failure hunted me for a long time.

SPACE MANAGEMENT

It is a lot easier to manage the parking space in the local church because the markings are already in place. Yet a problem could arise when ushers do not guide the people to park within the markings. Inexperienced drivers cannot ease in without taking more than their portion and as a result render the next lot unusable. An usher with driving skill should help those that have a problem parking into restricted spaces.

However, the situation is different when managing an open parking space at large meetings. Here, the organizers have to prepare an area for the purpose. Before the ushers' involvement, the organizing authority must have decided on the general approach to parking. Should they bring the cars within one parking area or have several areas? Should there be more than one entry and exit? Many factors determine the right approach. The choice depends on the volume of traffic, proximity of the parking lots to the venue, the nature of the nearest public highway and its effect on road users wanting to enter the parking lots. The Convention Planning Committee may have to consult the local government authority to avoid causing a traffic breach.

In 1998, a church in Lagos organized an all night power crusade just at the outskirts of the city. Well over two million people were expected. The traffic build up was such that the city became impassable six hours before the evening program. The situation did not improve until the greater part of the following day. It was a huge success but the traffic control and car parking failed completely.

With the decision on the location of parking lots, the ushers' responsibility is to plan the space for good use. If necessary, they should seek assistance from architects and those involved in traffic planning. They should define the internal circulation clearly and mark the lots boldly to guide cars for economic parking. It is worth emphasizing that people should not park without guidance; late comers, in a hurry to catch up with the meeting, would disorganize the parking arrangement if no one guides them.

In determining an appropriate parking method, the head usher should consider the ease of clearing the cars at the end of the meeting. It is, therefore, preferable to park cars back-to-back, rather than face-to-face. It takes less space to get a car back into the marking than to enter frontally.

Besides, the approach encourages the use of one lane driveway within the parking lot.

TRAFFIC FLOW

Clear definition of parking portions enhances the ease of traffic flow. This shows at the end of meeting, when more number of cars head toward the exit than did come in at any one time during the meeting. If the parking method does not allow cars backing out into the driveway, it would help avoid a lot of delays; the flow would be smooth.

It is good to have a oneway rather than a two-way drive within the parking lot. The former makes traffic flow in one way and creates fewer problems for the ushers. By leading toward separate exits, it paves the way for cars to move out of the parking lot more easily. It also reduces the traffic jam that usually builds up as people rush to leave at the end of meetings. At such times, ushers should clear the cars one sector after the other, starting with the one nearest to the exit.

Ushers should not, for any reason, allow parking along the drive. Apart from its negative effect on general flow of traffic, it limits the driveway and blocks other park users; it could cause a serious problem in time of emergency.

PART 4
WRAPPING UP

Ushering is not all about standing, walking around in the limelight, or just operating in the ministry of helps. Ushering is deeply spiritual, ministering to the Lord's people in the court of the King of kings. Being spiritual, it has its own hazards arising from the harassment of the enemy, the devil. So, the usher is in a spiritual battle. Ushering is not all about the stress associated with it. It has its own benefits, which are both material and spiritual. Like every other ministry, ushering has its pros and cons, too.

12
SPIRITUAL WARFARE FOR USHERS

Kingdom work is a spiritual battle and not a social outing. The enemy, the devil, makes this war inevitable because of his nature to oppose the work of God. So, whoever engages in God's work is automatically on a collision course with the devil. But it takes the spiritually minded to discern the satanic manipulations behind the worker's unpalatable physical experiences—fear, depression, weakness, and sickness.

We should note that Christian ushering is the maintenance of order at a spiritual meeting, and the devil, the god of disorder, will surely stand against the ushers. He [the devil] does this by sending his cohorts to manipulate the individuals in the congregation, create pockets of distraction, and introduce confusion. He might even affect physical things like the musical instruments, the lighting, and the public address system.

The usher deals with all manners of people that are under different spiritual influences. This assertion is in line with the Scriptures where the apostle John advises that we should test every spirit to know whether it is from God (1 John 4:1). He goes further to strengthen believers by saying,

> *"You have already won your fight with these false prophets, because the Spirit who lives in you is greater than the spirit who lives in the world." (1 John 4:4 NLT)*

The spiritual principle behind these Scriptures goes this way: The believer receives the Spirit of God the moment he or she accepts Jesus Christ as Lord and Savior (Galatians 4:6). It follows that without the Spirit of Christ one easily comes under Satan's manipulation. Equally, a believer that is not strong in Christ is open to the devil's control.

So the usher has two groups of people to contend with: those that live by the spirit of the world and those that are not spiritually strong in Christ. The enemy can affect the meeting through any of these two. The spiritual warfare, therefore, is not against the human person but against the spirit behind the person's behavior. Consequently, the usher should not rest on just being aware of the spiritual basis of physical happenings. He should have a deeper and precise knowledge of satanic operations and be able to address the demon spirit behind a specific issue. It is pure spiritual naivety to ignore the devil's antics or presume that he is not interested in the meeting. But the enemy likes to shroud his activities to have his way. Thus, he is always livid with rage whenever the Holy Spirit exposes him.

The enemy targets the usher, the organizers of the function, the officiating ministers, the musical instruments, and the congregation at large. The usher is a target because he is the first point of contact—a conspicuous one, for that matter. The enemy knows that by destabilizing the usher, he disorganizes the meeting. For example, there will be a communication breakdown if the ushers start bickering against each other; the right team spirit gives way. Again, if an usher reacts noisily against an unruly behavior by a member of the congregation, his action distracts other people within his section.

So the enemy operates in different ways but for the same purpose of disrupting the meeting. Apart from upsetting the usher, the enemy uses other covert means to operate with and cause confusion, disorder, rebellion, contention and strife, distractions, mind control, slumber, and seduction of all sorts. But, with the help of the Holy Spirit (1 Corinthians 12:10) and experience, the usher should be able to identify the nature of spirit in operation; he has a divine mandate to exercise spiritual authority over the meeting and over individuals at the meeting. This is the only way to accomplish his mission; and he wins the battle on his knees before the function. Thus, he does not issue his own instructions but Christ's, and when he acts in love, the people must comply. But his legitimacy in exercising spiritual authority depends on his relationship with Jesus Christ. If he deliberately lives in sin, the demons will search it out and use it as a basis for flouting of his directives. But if he is sure of his relationship with the Lord, he should confront every situation boldly, trusting the Lord's total protection and support.

> *And they shall fight against thee; but they shall not prevail against thee; for I am with thee, saith the Lord, to deliver thee. (Jeremiah 1:19)*

A word of caution: Every movement that causes distraction is not necessarily satanic. The usher should be mindful of the spirit of suspicion, which makes him see every move as coming from the enemy. He should be able to judge, assess, and evaluate the nature of every spirit to know whether it is from God. He should able to differentiate natural human behavior from satanic manifestation.

ESSENTIAL STEPS FOR WARFARE

An usher should cultivate sound spiritual disciplines as part of his or her normal Christian life. These include meditating on God's word, prayer and fasting, praying in tongues, and living conscious of one's standing in Christ. Practise of spiritual discipline makes him alert always, especially during ministrations.

Prophetic Affirmation of God's Word.

A believer's spiritual authority is related to his understanding of God's word. God has a right word for every situation in life, and by their correct use, the believer strengthens his or her faith and boldness in battle. He should find out what the Lord says about him and the enemy, and stand on them. Such Scriptures should form the basis for regular positive affirmative statements. For example:

➢ I have power over the enemy.

Behold, I give unto you power to tread on serpents and scorpions, and over all the power of the enemy: and nothing shall by any means hurt you. (Luke 10:19)

➢ The Lord has placed me over every form of evil spirit.

Who hath delivered us from the power of darkness, and hath translated us into the kingdom of his dear Son. (Colossians 1:13)

➢ I am in Christ; therefore, the enemy cannot reach me.

For ye are dead, and your life is hid with Christ in God. (Colossians 3:3)

➢ The Lord has strengthened me for the battle; victory is mine.

For thou hast girded me with strength unto the battle: thou hast subdued under me those that rose up against me. (Psalm 18:39)

➢ I have a divine shield of protection from the enemy's fiery darts.

Thou hast also given me the shield of thy salvation: and thy right hand hath holden me up, and thy gentleness hath made me great. (Psalm 18:35)

And take the helmet of salvation, and the sword of the Spirit, which is the word of God. (Ephesians 6:17)

➢ I have the right to pronounce judgment on the enemies of this meeting.

Let the high praises of God be in their mouth, and a twoedged sword in their hand; To execute vengeance upon the heathen, and punishments upon the people; To bind their kings with chains, and their nobles with fetters of iron; To execute upon them the judgment written: this honour have all his saints. Praise ye the Lord. (Psalm 149:6-9)

Exercising Spiritual Authority

An interesting aspect of spiritual warfare is that divine missiles do not respect time or distance; they always hit their target, in the power of the Holy Spirit. Ushers make use of this wonderful opportunity to take over the venue spiritually even before the function. How?

➢ Paralyse the controlling spirits with fear of the Lord.

And she said unto the men, I know that the Lord hath given you the land, and that your terror is fallen upon us, and that all the inhabitants of the land faint because of you. For we have heard how the Lord dried up the water of the Red sea for you, when ye came out of Egypt; and what ye did unto the two kings of the Amorites, that were on the other side Jordan, Sihon and Og, whom ye utterly destroyed. And as soon as we had heard these things, our hearts did melt, neither did there remain any more courage in any man, because of you: for the Lord your God, he is God in heaven above, and in earth beneath. (Joshua 2:9-11)

➢ Scatter all the demon spirits that have gathered against the Lord's work.

Associate yourselves, O ye people, and ye shall be broken in pieces; and give ear, all ye of far countries: gird yourselves, and ye shall be broken in pieces;

gird yourselves, and ye shall be broken in pieces. Take counsel together, and it shall come to nought; speak the word, and it shall not stand: for God is with us. (Isaiah 8:9-10)

➢ Nullify and turn their wise counsel to foolishness.

And David said, O Lord, I pray thee, turn the counsel of Ahithophel into foolishness. (2 Samuel 15:31)

➢ Ask that the light of Christ should cover the venue of the meeting and disperse every form of darkness.

And the Lord will create upon every dwelling place of mount Zion, and upon her assemblies, a cloud and smoke by day, and the shining of a flaming fire by night: for upon all the glory shall be a defence. (Isaiah 4:5)

➢ Ask God to create a cloud and a smoke by day upon the place of meeting and the shining of flaming fire by night.

And there shall be a tabernacle for a shadow in the daytime from the heat, and for a place of refuge, and for a covert from storm and from rain. (Isaiah 4:6)

> Finally, ask God to purge and fan out every demon spirit that is in hiding.

Moreover the Lord thy God will send the hornet among them, until they that are left, and hide themselves from thee, be destroyed. (Deuteronomy 7:20)

During ministration, each usher has his own zone of authority. He should, prophetically, announce his presence, establish his standard, and control the zone. He should speak to the seats commanding them not to harbor any agents of darkness, but reject the enemy's move to use them against their maker. In principle, the whole creation, including the seats, is made by the word of God; they hear and obey God's word when spoken with Christ's authority. God created them for His glory and the usher should direct them to do God's will for their existence. This should follow the spiritual principle in the Bible where God directed His prophets to speak to the mountains or the land.

Part of establishing spiritual authority is to carry out a prophetic prayer walk around the venue of meeting. This is a very serious spiritual exercise, during which the ushers physically define their zone of spiritual control. It is prophetic because the Lord directs them on what pronouncements to make and the right timing for making them. In such a warfare, one does not add to or subtract from the Lord's directive. Joshua's experience in the battle against Jericho stands out as a good example. He did just what the Lord commanded him to do. The head usher should lead such an exercise.

Dealing with Controlling Spirits

It is good to address Satan's agents by their names, if such are known. With prayer and as one grows in the work of ushering, the Holy Spirit could disclose names of specific demons at work. Pastor John J Eckhardt[6] lists some of the spirits as follows:

- *Carbolla*: Controls human will. There are people that would like to accept Christ but lack the will to do so. This is the operation of the evil spirit who restrains such people from having a desire for Christ and His word. Conversely, the Holy Spirit gives the believer the desire to obey God and the power to do His will (Philippians 2:13).
- *Galendo*: Controls false tongues. Satan's agents speak in false tongues mainly to cause confusion and hide comfortably in the midst of believers. The damsel's utterances, though in plain speech, confused the apostle Paul and his team for some time before he [Paul] discerned the spirit acting through her (Acts 16:16-18).
- *Jurver:* Controls the human mind. It causes distraction, mind blocking, and lack of concentration (2 Corinthians 4:3-4) that people experience during meetings.

- *Megancardioni:* Causes confusion of speech. This spirit ensures that the speaker does not put across his message coherently and convincingly to his audience. The Bible records that God sent the spirit of Babel (confusion) to disorganize and frustrate man's attempt at building a tower that would reach heaven (Genesis 11). So, Babel is another name for the spirit of confusion.
- *Sesilus:* Causes contention and strife. This spirit works to destabilize the ushering team or any other Christian group. This same spirit is revealed in Genesis 26:20 as Esek. It causes such non-Christian behavior as fighting, bickering, quarrelling, and struggling for positions and honor in the church.
- *Varrier*: Responsible for disobedience, rebellion, stubbornness, insubordination, and witchcraft. It operates more among the youths in the church.

Maintaining Spiritual Alertness

It is essential to maintain spiritual alertness by focusing on the day's ministration. The mind wanders when the usher becomes an attendee rather than a minister—a form of sleeping on duty. Spiritual alertness makes him receptive to the prompting of the Holy Spirit. Thus, he could easily preempt the enemy's attempt at creating pockets of distractions. There is no better way of staying alert than by praying in tongues and interceding for different segments of the meeting. It is better to pray through the meeting.

For example, while preparing for a Full Gospel Business Men's Fellowship International Convention meeting in 1996, I fasted and prayed extensively for the ushering ministration. Just before the start of meeting, the Lord revealed, in a dream, a heavily built man who walked into the gathering and challenged my authority as the head usher. During the meeting proper, at the closing rally, a heavily built man actually came late in the program and insisted on seeing the guest speaker. I tried, however courteously, to make him understand that my agreeing to his request would cause distraction. In spite of my attempt, he remained adamant and challenged my authority to deny him entry. I immediately recalled the revelation and had to call in the police. I later discovered that the intruder travelled quite a distance to come to the meeting, but he could not give any convincing reason why he insisted on seeing the speaker. Through prayer, the usher sees beyond the physical and interprets the happenings at a meeting from the spiritual point of view.

The most crucial time for spiritual alertness is during deliverance ministration. At such times, the enemy fights back by sending out his fiery darts—his reaction against the manifestation of Christ's power to save and deliver people under his grip. He could be violent, at times, or express his anger in other ways. For example, one can experience a sudden surge of lustful feelings on getting close to a member of the opposite sex; this indicates the attack of a seducing spirit.

Some years back, a minor drama erupted in the church at the end of a Sunday worship service. Two women members of the choir, very committed ones, behaved in a way that attracted the attention of the pastors. As the church gathered to pray for them, we observed signs of demonic manifestation in them. There was a strange display of physical strength, fighting back every attempt by the men to hold them down. During the more than 90 minutes deliverance ministration, they 'vomited' a lot of obscenities one should not expect from Christians. It was like exposing some secret unchristian behavior of some members of the leadership. The two women never came back to the church after that episode.

Ushers should know that when a spiritual environment is positively charged with the Holy Spirit anointing, the devil's agents can react in a violent manner. The above scene shows that the enemy knows every worker's spiritual state and lifestyle. Sin is the devil's trademark, and whoever has it cannot boldly challenge him [Satan], or claim to be on the side of Christ's kingdom. In effect, the one has no moral justification for fighting against the devil. Satan reacts angrily against those who, through their lifestyle, belong to his camp but still turn against him. Christ said,

And if Satan rise up against himself, and be divided, he cannot stand, but hath an end. (Mark 3:26)

The usher should not only be alert while ministering

but should also be careful with his or her spiritual purity. Those who see the ministry as a mere social outing run the risk of exposing themselves to danger. Such people could go through some inexplicable experiences in life, the cause of which they will not be able to discover.

Handling A Backlash

The fact that the enemy did not fight back during the function does not mean that all is over. He does not easily give up but might wait for a time when the usher's spiritual guard is low and attack in form of general body weakness, pains, sleeplessness, depression, and terrifying nightmares. Though the ushering team must have prayed at the end of the meeting, one should not be hasty to go to sleep. Rather, he should put the enemy on the defensive with affirmations and decrees that draw from God's word.

13
BENEFITS OF USHERING

Kingdom work attracts benefits and rewards. God is not a taskmaster who extracts labor without minding the welfare of the laborer; He blesses those that willingly serve Him. The benefits of ushering are both material and spiritual. Whichever, they confirm God's faithfulness in repaying every genuine labor.

Therefore, my beloved brethren, be ye stedfast, unmovable, always abounding in the work of the Lord, forasmuch as ye know that your labour is not in vain in the Lord. (1 Corinthians 15:58)

MATERIAL BENEFITS

There are many material benefits of ushering and these show as one grows in the ministry. Interestingly, the benefits affect his or her personality, thus impacting his social life.

New People Skills

Social interaction is easier and smoother within the same interest group. Ushering helps the individual interact with more groups and classes of people than he ordinarily would. In the process, he develops a 'new people skills', the art of relating freely with unfamiliar persons by making them feel at home and comfortable. As the usher unconsciously radiates genuine love toward others, he endears to them and breaks any form of social barriers and inhibitions. So, ushering helps the usher develop the habit of:

➤ Matching names with faces.
➤ Learning and recalling new names and faces
➤ Making new friends easily.

In the ministry, everybody sees the usher and expects him to know them. By matching a name with the face, he would break the wall of social separation and win the person's heart. First time worshippers feel at home and relate with an amiable usher. I have heard testimonies of people that would have left a church but for the way the ushers related to them at first contact. There are also instances where lasting relationships resulted from good ushering.

Good Encourager

The usher attracts people because of his cheerful and amiable disposition. This is an asset in an increasingly individualistic society, where people have a problem finding whom to relate with. As the usher comes across different faces and moods, he could discern their problems and drop a relevant Scripture to make the person's day. People that are hurting usually get a big relief from such an encounter. They would like to get closer to the usher, feeling free to discuss their personal problems and seek counsel. I have seen it work in lifting the mood of many.

Order In Personal Life

God orders the lives of those that maintain order in His house. A committed and diligent usher organizes his life and work more readily. With time, his life becomes more purposeful as order shows in his personal appearance.

Wholesome Personality

The mark of a wholesome personality is the ability to relate decently with all manner of people. Being a ministry of help, it enables the usher relate with various types of characters at different social levels. He combines firmness with humility in attending to people, and when done with decent cheerfulness, he develops a winsome personality.

SPIRITUAL BENEFITS

Spiritual benefits of ushering show up over time in the usher's character, indicating how much of spiritual values he or she has inculcated. However, it is humanly impossible to evaluate the amount of spiritual benefits one gets from doing the kingdom work. But a few of the noticeable benefits should illustrate the point.

Personal Witnessing

Ushering teaches the art of applying the right word about Jesus to different people at different occasions. It imparts an amiable disposition, which helps him or her to easily initiate a lively discussion with a new person. Naturally, strangers feel more disposed to listen to the witnessing of Christ if they are relaxed with the presenter. Therefore, the ministry improves the usher's personal witnessing skill.

Spiritual Growth

Ushering helps the worker to be focused and committed. And the regular habit of taking the problem of ministry to the Lord, in prayer and study of the Word, deepens his spiritual growth and maturity. Ushering enables the individual develop essential Christian virtues like humility, meekness, love, temperance, and faithfulness. As he interacts with people, these virtues have positive effect on them. In other words, he imparts grace on others, thereby edifying the Body of Christ.

Spiritual Promotion

It opens opportunities to other ministries the usher might not have known he could operate in. For example, praying for people and situations in the church could lead the usher to the ministry of intercession. Philip, the evangelist, started as an usher but ended as a first century notable evangelist. Believers should know that what looks like a "low level office" in God's work is an essential stepping stone to higher assignments. God trusts the one that is faithful in a "small" position has the required discipline for higher positions.

> *His lord said unto him, Well done, good and faithful servant; thou hast been faithful over a few things, I will make thee ruler over many things: enter thou into the joy of thy lord. (Matthew 25:23)*

Personal Fulfilment

It leads to a fulfilling Christian life. The usher finds himself or herself relevant to the church and to God. With such feeling of relevance, one grows in excellence in ministry, knowing that the work belongs to the Lord, who loves excellence and perfection.

It is a known spiritual fact that God does not reward an office or position, but diligence and commitment. He rewards and promotes workers on the basis of their identification with and commitment to His program. Part of the secrets of spiritual success is to begin one's Christian service in those areas that would help one develop the virtues of meekness and humility. There is no better place to start than in the ministry of ushering.

14
PROBLEMS OF USHERING

The Bible reveals that one's ministry provides the enemy the basis for spiritual attack and temptation. For example, if Jesus Christ were not a 'teacher come from God', the Jewish leaders would not have accused Him with trump-up charges. The same applied to the apostle Paul. The usher, therefore, should find out the problems associated with his or her ministry and avoid the pitfalls.

It is worth mentioning that high rate of mobility is a problem that plagues the ushering ministry in most of the churches. Head ushers, because of their proven commitment to duty, easily grow out of their ministry. This is evident mainly in the fast growing churches where there is an ever-pressing need for pastors. No sooner has the head usher settled down to function than the church ordains and posts him to pastor a new parish. This practice disorganizes the team and affects its effectiveness. I believe that with some creativity, a head usher could still fit into the church hierarchy and serve in his area of calling.

STUNTED SPIRITUALITY

Ushering could divert one's attention from true Christian spirituality. The usher is busy with keeping order at meetings or during worship services without being part of the spiritual activity of the day; he is just present physically but not intimately involved spiritually. He does not follow the teaching of the day, does not participate in the prayers. This does a lot of harm to his spiritual life.

However, the head usher could get around this problem by devising ways and means of enriching the spiritual quality of his team. The regular ushers' meetings provide ample opportunity for doing so; he uses such occasions to teach and exhort them and take them through the Sunday school lesson of the following church worship service. Ushers should receive tape recordings of teaching at large meetings. On his own, the usher should find other means of maintaining sound spiritual growth by attending meetings where he does not minister.

WRONG PERCEPTION OF CHRISTIAN LIFE

We mentioned earlier that the ministry puts the usher in the limelight. If the usher does not handle the exposure carefully, he may stay on in the ministry because of the glamor without counting the spiritual cost. He would think that Christianity is all about social acceptance. When he sees ushering as a means of widening his social and business connections, he could go out of the way to exploit this wide range of opportunities the ministry exposes him to. There is nothing wrong in expanding one's social and business contacts within the Christian fold provided it does not redirect the focus of one's purpose for kingdom service. This could mean exploitation and perversion.

GIFT-CHARACTER MIX

At times, the usher's glamorous externals could take him faster to higher appointments. In such a case, he grows in service without growing in Christian character and spirituality. The damage does not show easily until a situation that tests his character arises. An embarrassing gap would then open up to reveal his true level of spiritual maturity in relation to his reputation as a gifted usher.

PERSONAL INTEGRITY

Many ushers have been caught dipping into the church collections, a common temptation that puts the usher's personal integrity to the test. More often some ushers put their monetary needs above the fear of the Lord and fall to the urge to 'help-themselves-a-little' with church collections. It is the head usher's duty to find ways, through prayer, of reducing such temptations by devising checks and balances in money handling. Good advice is not to involve the unemployed in counting and recording collections without good supervision. In effect, the head usher should monitor collections strictly.

MORAL VALUES

Ushering ministry has a good number of young Christians—both in age and in spiritual maturity. Without enforcing discipline and strict moral values, the spirit of immorality could creep in and pollute both the group and the church. The head usher should discourage situations that would expose the team to any form of immorality. His intercessory prayers for the members could help him identify and nip such problems in the bud. He should also watch out for members that bask in glamor and socials, and do not show promise for spirituality. Such are likely sources of moral pollution of the team.

SPIRITUAL ATTACK

The ministry exposes the ushers to different forms of spiritual attacks, which could come in different forms and guises—stunted spiritual growth, moral laxity, pilfering, and indiscipline. Corporate intercessory prayers for members of the team can be of immense help in this regard.

15
USHER'S QUICK REFERENCE

1. How will I know that I can function as an usher?
   - *a*   *You are not pleased when things are done in a disorderly manner.*
   - *b*   *You like to dress smartly and decently most of the time.*
   - *c*   *You are sociable and interact with others freely.*
2. What personal qualities should I need as an usher?
   - *a*   *Love for people and friendliness.*
   - *b*   *Sense of humor.*
   - *c*   *Tact in handling people and situations.*
   - *d*   *Keen sense of observation and good memory.*
   - *e*   *It reflects the image of your church or organization.*
   - *f*   *It could make you too self-conscious, thus hindering your effectiveness.*

6. How should I dress as an usher?
    a   *Dress smart and simple. Ensure that your dressing fits your natural figure.*
    b   *You don't need to be trendy to appear smart.*
    c   *Do not dress to distract or seduce.*
    d   *Let not your dressing hinder your ease of movement.*
7. How does personal hygiene affect ushering?
    a   *People react to 'Body Odor' and 'Bad Breath'. Pay regular visit to the dentist.*
    b   *Wear mild perfume after a regular bath.*
8. How do I receive people at meetings?
    a   *Radiate warm infectious smile.*
    b   *Never wear a long face of depressing look.*
    c   *Look at people in the eye when greeting people. Don't look down or look the other way.*
9. How do I seat people at meetings?
    a   *Do not point but walk them to their seats. Or politely direct them to the nearest usher that would lead them to their seats.*
    b   *Seat people in such a way as to cause minimal discomfort to those already seated.*
    c   *Seat people from front row to back row.*
    d   *Seat people from centre to the aisle or from end to the aisle.*
10. Some people are simply unpleasant. How do I

handle them?
- *a* *Love them. Your duty is to help people enjoy the meeting.*
- *b* *Be ever polite but pray for them inwardly.*

11. How do I handle difficult people?
    - *a* *Always see people's problems from the spiritual point of view.*
    - *b* *Intercede and take control of whatever spirit that controls their lives.*
    - *c* *Don't insist on getting even with a difficult person. It could lead to distraction.*
    - *d* *Allow the person sit wherever he would want to, if possible.*
    - *e* *Familiarize with such people and gradually win their love and respect.*

12. How do I control my section?
    - *a* *Maintain constant prayer and physical vigilance.*
    - *b* *Take spiritual control of your section through prophetic pronouncements.*
    - *c* *When seated, occasionally run your eyes over your section watching out for movement or people that may need your attention.*

13. Should an usher always walk around and not have a seat?
    - *a* *The usher should sit at the first seat of the last row of his section, and along the aisle.*
    - *b* *He should walk around when the need*

arises—offering, head counts etc.

    c   People feel bad if an usher blocks their view.

14. What is the fastest way to collect offering?
    - *a   Be ready for offering well ahead of time.*
    - *b   Start collecting from the front and move towards the last row.*
    - *c   Let people observe the movement of offering bags before it gets to them.*
    - *d   Politely nudge people to speed up if there is a delay down the row.*
    - *e   Visually follow the movement of the bag.*

15. How do I ensure effective collection?
    - *a   Ensure that there are enough offering bags, and note the number given out.*
    - *b   Have the bags evenly distributed through the meeting.*
    - *c   Do not allow people to dip into the bags.*
    - *d   Ensure the number of bags returned at the end tallies with the number given out.*
    - *e   Assign the duty of counting and recording to mature ushers.*

16. What is the easiest way to conduct attendance count?
    - *a   Work with the seats within your section.*
    - *b   Count the empty seats and subtract the number from the total seats.*
    - *c   Count the second time and take the average.*

17. How do I ensure smooth flow during special ministrations?
    - *a   Position yourself before commencement of ministration.*
    - *b   Channel the people to the altar through the primary aisles.*
    - *c   Lead them back to their seats through the secondary aisles.*
    - *d   Do not let the altar congest more than necessary.*
    - *e   Engage additional ushers from other sections to assist.*
    - *f   Carry out those that fall under anointing.*
18. How do I assist a person that is being ministered to?
    - *a   Ensure that an usher assists a person of the same sex.*
    - *b   Do not stand behind a person much taller or heavier than you are.*
    - *c   Maintain a good distance such that you would be able to break the fall effectively.*
    - *d   Safeguard the person's personal effects that are prone to damage.*
    - *e   Use a headgear to protect a woman's decency.*
19. How do I prepare for emergency?
    - *a   Expect emergency situations to arise.*
    - *b   Locate emergency exit points before commencement of meeting.*
    - *c   Identify the locations of fire fighting*

        appliances before the meeting.
- *d   Clear the aisles of any obstructions.*
- *e   Do not allow seats outside authorized areas.*

20. What should I do in time of emergency?
    - *a   Be calm, but at alert.*
    - *b   Identify the source of cause of panic.*
    - *c   Use the public address system to communicate with the people.*
    - *d   Lead the people away from the likely source of cause of panic.*

21. What do I need to know about the venue?
    - *a   Identify locations of activity centers.*
    - *b   Imagine likely questions members of the congregation would ask and have your answers ready.*

22. How do I avoid Fire Brigade approach to ushering ministration?
    - *a   Plan well ahead of time.*
    - *b   Have all material requirements ready, and put in places where you would need them.*
    - *c   Work ahead of the program, and be ready well before an item comes up.*

23. How can I enhance my endurance limit during ushering?
    - *a   Train for physical strength through jogging and some indoor exercises.*
    - *b   Develop good standing habit with body weight well distributed down the frame—*

always stand erect.
- *c   Do not stand in the same posture for a long time. Occasionally stand on your toes in order to ease tension at the ankles.*
- *d   Form the habit of deep and regular breathing to ensure copious intake of oxygen. This helps avoid dizziness and fatigue.*

24. What should be the usher's prayer focus?
- *a   Ask the Holy Spirit for wisdom, discernment, boldness, and excellence.*
- *b   Ask God to equip you with His whole armor.*
- *c   Pray for spiritual empowerment for the work.*
- *d   Pray for other members of team and for the meeting.*

25. What should be the targets of spiritual warfare?

Battle against the following: the spirits of hindrance, distraction, rebellion, disorder and confusion, strife and contention, and seduction.

26. How can I know that I am under spiritual attack?

Watch out for the following:
- *a   A sudden feeling of weakness and exhaustion.*
- *b   A sudden feeling of fear or panic.*
- *c   A momentary feeling of confusion and lack of coordination of actions.*
- *d   If you feel sexually aroused at the nearness of the opposite sex.*

- e *If you feel an unusual loss of peace and composure.*
- f *If you experience a nightmare in the sleep just after the ministration.*
- g *If you observe awkward occurrences around your home.*

27. What is the meaning of a spiritual backlash?

Backlash is the spiritual attack that comes on the usher after the end of an outing. It may be through nightmares in the dream, and other awkward bodily and emotional reactions and feelings.

28. How do I improve my effectiveness?
    - a *Regard ushering as your ministry; let it be a main focus of prayer.*
    - b *Study the Bible with a genuine intention to improve in your Christian life, and in the ministry.*
    - c *Observe mature ushers minister.*
    - d *Read to improve your understanding of human and crowd behavior.*
    - e *Work on your weak areas in human relation.*
    - f *Train your power of observation to sharpen your sensitivity.*

29. Explain the meaning of body language in ushering.
    - a *Body language is a means of communicating with other members of the team without causing distraction to the congregation. Functioning as a team,*

ushers evolve subtle methods of communicating with each other.

    b   *They learn them during training sessions, but internalize them in the course of ministering together. Such tools include the head, hands, and finger and eye movements.*

30. How should I relate to other ushers?
    a   *They are your partners in service; your success depends on them.*
    b   *Resolve not to be a source of strife and contention in the team.*
    c   *Love them and socialize freely with them.*
    d   *Pray for each member of the team.*
    e   *Avoid gossiping and backbiting.*

31. How do I minister without missing the teachings of the day?
    a   *Get a ready supply of your ushering needs before the start of meeting.*
    b   *Do not move around without a cogent reason to do so.*
    c   *Take short notes of key points during teachings.*
    d   *Study the Bible regularly for deeper understanding.*

32. What is the usher's source of joy in the ministry?
    God has graciously called you to work with Him.

33. Will I be an usher all my Christian life?
    a   *Yes, if the Lord says so.*
    b   *No, if the Lord has another ministry for you. This means that He uses ushering as a stepping-stone to other responsibilities.*
34. When does ushering function start and end?
    a   *The nature of meeting determines how long it would take the ushers to prepare. Coming early enables the ushers put things in place; pray for corporately for the meeting.*
    b   *It ends as soon as the congregation has left, records are entered, and the hall is made ready for the following day's function, if necessary.*
35. How can an usher evaluate his or her spiritual life?
    a   *Do I really show genuine love to the people I minister to?*
    b   *Do I radiate that joy directly from my heart, or is it mechanical?*
    c) *Am I patient with all classes of people I minister to, or do I treat people selectively?*
    d   *Do I go the extra mile in showing kindness to members of the congregation?*
    e   *Do I take extra pains in fulfilling my promises to members of the congregation?*
    h   *Am I more attracted by the material benefits of ushering than the joy of serving*

the Lord?

i How far have I fared in my spiritual life— in prayer, worship and reading of the Word?

NOTES

[1] Charles Sibthorpe. *Authority—the Imperative for Christian Leaders* (Highland Books. 1996). Pg. 18

[2] Dr Sidney N. Bremer. *Successful Achievement* (Academy of Successful Achievement, South Carolina. 1966). Vol. 2, pg. 549

[3] Peter Wiwcharuck. *Building Effective Leadership* (International Leadership Development Foundation. 1988). Pg. 20.

[4] Sol Stein. *Solutions for Writers* (Souvenir Press Ltd. 2001). Pg 12.

[5] Buddy Bell. *The Complete Local Church Usher's Handbook* (Harrison House, Inc. 1996). Pg. 4851.

[6] John J. Eckhardt. *Deliverance and Spiritual Warfare Manual* (Noade Nigeria Ltd, 1988). Pg 20.

Made in the USA